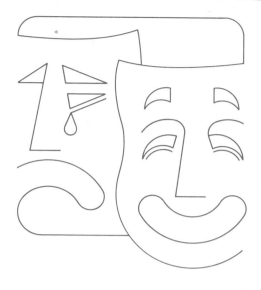

WORLD OF CULTURE

THEATER

by Jacques Burdick

Newsweek Books, New York

NEWSWEEK BOOKS

Joseph L. Gardner, Editor

Janet Czarnetzki, Art Director
Edwin D. Bayrd, Jr., Associate Editor
Ellen Kavier, Researcher-Writer
Elaine Andrews, Copy Editor

S. Arthur Dembner, President

ARNOLDO MONDADORI EDITORE

Giuliana Nannicini, Editor

Mariella De Battisti, Picture Researcher
Marisa Melis, Editorial Secretary
Enrico Segré, Designer
Giovanni Adamoli, Production Coordinator

Grateful acknowledgment is made for the use of excerpted material on pages 154-177 from the following works:

Act One by Moss Hart. Copyright © 1959 by Catherine Carlisle Hart and Joseph M. Hyman, Trustees. Reprinted by permission of Random House, Inc.

A Gift of Joy by Helen Hayes and Lewis Funke. Copyright © 1965 by Helen Hayes and Lewis Funke. Reprinted by permission of the publisher, M. Evans & Company, Inc.

Don't Put Your Daughter on the Stage by Margaret Webster. Copyright © 1962, 1972 by Margaret Webster. Reprinted by permission of Alfred A. Knopf, Inc.

George S. Kaufman: An Intimate Portrait by Howard Teichman. Copyright © 1972 by Howard Teichman. Reprinted by permission of Atheneum Publishers.

Laurette by Marguerite Courtney. Copyright © 1955 by Marguerite Courtney. Reprinted by permission of Lucy Kroll Agency.

Notes on a Cowardly Lion by John Lahr. Copyright © 1969 by John Lahr. Reprinted by permission of Alfred A. Knopf, Inc.

People in a Diary: A Memoir by S.N. Behrman. Copyright © 1972 by S.N. Behrman. Reprinted by permission of Little, Brown and Company.

Pieces at Eight by Walter Kerr. Copyright © 1952, 1957 by Walter Kerr. Published in 1968 by E.P. Dutton & Co., Inc. in a paperback edition and used with their permission. This selection originally appeared in the *New York Herald Tribune*.

Tallulah by Brendan Gill. Copyright © 1972 by Brendan Gill. Reprinted by permission of Holt, Rinehart and Winston, Inc.

The Art of Night, from *The Magic Mirror* by George Jean Nathan. Copyright © 1960 by Alfred A. Knopf, Inc. Reprinted by permission of the publisher.

The Magic Curtain by Lawrence Langner. Copyright © 1951 by Lawrence Langner. Reprinted by permission of Armina Marshall.

ISBN: Regular edition 0-88225-103-1 ISBN: Deluxe edition 0-88225-104-x
Library of Congress Catalog Card No. 73-89392
©1974 Europa Verlag. All rights reserved.
Printed and bound by Mondadori, Verona, Italy

Contents

1

Imitation and Celebration

THE UNWRITTEN HISTORY of theater is the history of mankind, for in its essentials that set of human actions which the ancient Greeks formalized as *theater* belongs to no single race, age, or culture. It is, rather, an act of language, one by which the dangerous phenomenal world is safely imitated and celebrated. This act, lying as it does at the very heart of ritual, has been common to all men—albeit in varying degrees —since man was created. The sorcerer imitating the stag–in a scene painted on the wall of a cave–and the Broadway actor imitating Sir Winston Churchill—in a scene photographed for a recent playbill— have a common bond in spite of the twenty thousand years of actual time that divide them.

A comprehensive history of the theater would, of necessity, fill many volumes and require lengthy contributions from experts in a dozen disciplines, among them literature, history, archaeology, psychology, sociology, anthropology, and religion. The purpose of this volume, then, is to present the world of theater in overview—showing, in an admittedly cursory manner, how theater, one of the most sensitive indices of man's cultural development, perpetually alters its form, develops, declines, and rediscovers its sources.

The history of theater in Europe begins in Athens more than five and a half centuries before the birth of Christ. There, in a tiny, bowl-like hollow, their backs protected from the cold winds of Mount Parnes and the bright morning sun, Athenians celebrated those rites of the god Dionysus that were to evolve into theater—one of the greatest cultural accomplishments of the Greeks. Indeed, this new art was so intimately associated with Greek civilization that every major town and colony possessed a theater, the quality of the building itself being an index of the settlement's importance.

Greek dramatic masks revealed both a character's sex and mood. This gold pendant, a miniature of the somewhat standardized tragic mask, presents the face of a querulous woman.

The Greek theater—or, more precisely, that form of theater we have come to know as tragedy—seems to have originated in the dithyramb, a kind of dance performed in honor of the god Dionysus. Since Dionysus was the deity of wine and fertility, it is not surprising that dances dedicated to him tended to be disorderly and the dancers drunk. By the end of the seventh century B.C., performances of the dithyramb had spread from Sicyon in the Dorian lands of the Peloponnesus, where they are said to have originated, to the area around Corinth, where they gained literary prominence. Soon they had spread to Thebes and to the islands of Paros and Naxos. For those who have seen the remarkable effects of Greek sunshine, a little resinated wine, and that spontaneous good humor called *kefi*, it is not difficult to understand how this early round dance achieved widespread popularity, with revelers celebrating the mysteries of vinous liberation.

Nothing in the formality and refinement of the dramatic productions of Periclean Athens resembled the drunken, disorderly fertility rites of two centuries earlier. Greek drama had originated in those rites however—a fact attested to by the very terms *tragedy* and *comedy*. The word *tragedy*—from *tragos*, "goat," and *odé*, "song"—literally harks back to the village dithyrambs, in which the performers wore goatskins and capered about like goats, and at which a kid was often the prize for the best performance. And although Aristotle disagrees, there is little doubt that *comedy* derives from *kômazein*, "to wander around villages" —suggesting that the performers, because of their bawdy rowdiness, had been forbidden to perform in the city.

In the sixth century, Thespis, a lyric poet who traveled by cart from village to village organizing celebrations for local feasts, intro-

Originally a circular, paved threshing floor, the theater orchestra gradually became semicircular. The raised stage of Athens' famous Theater of Dionysus, whose ruins are shown at left, was probably not built until the theater was remodeled in Roman times. A detail from a fifth-century krater painting (right) shows Clytemnestra's lover, Aegisthus, slaying her husband, Agamemnon—a familiar Greek tale that was dramatized by Aeschylus in his celebrated Oresteia *trilogy.*

duced the dithyramb to Attica. No longer disorderly dances performed by bawling tipplers, the dithyrambs Thespis wrote, directed, and starred in were well-organized productions of literary texts, danced and sung to the accompaniment of a flute by fifty men or boys.

It was either Thespis or his successor, Phrynichus, who, by distinguishing one performer from the rest of the chorus—thus creating the necessity for dramatic dialogue—invented the form known as tragedy. The new form received official approbation in 538 B.C., when the tyrant Pisistratus ordered the first Athenian competition for tragedy. Its introduction as a civic competition elevated the new form of cele-

bration to the sacred cultural status of the Athenian games. Pisistratus further insured its permanence by assigning it a precinct in a busy sector of the city, a slope between the steep south escarpment of the upper city and the Street of Tripods. The land was consecrated to the god Dionysus, and to this day it is known as the Theater of Dionysus.

Nothing remains of the earliest structures used as theaters, although scholars, using bits of information gathered from many sources, have pieced together a reliable composite portrait of those edifices. We know, for instance, that from the very beginning the principal feature of the performing area was the circular orchestra (from *orcheisthai*, "to

The chorus danced and chanted in the orchestra, but the actors declaimed from a separate section, the skene. In the beginning these simple settings were built of wood, as this fragment from a vase painting indicates. A side wing of the skene proper, the parakaskenion, was surmounted by a roof capped with statues.

10

dance"), where the chorus danced and sang. It is probable that the round, paved areas that rural communities throughout Greece still use for threshing were, because of their shape and availability, the first orchestras—a term that in certain European theaters still designates an area that can be cleared of seats and used for social dancing. Adjacent to this area were an altar to the gods; a tithing house, where offerings were received and kept; and a tiring house, where the performers dressed and from which they proceeded to the circular dancing ground. Both the tithing house and the tiring house were constructed of wood. It is also likely that the Athenian audience, too numerous to stand, sat upon ramps of earth heaped up around the orchestra. Later, wooden bleachers were constructed over these ramps to facilitate seating.

The theater building we now think of as typically Greek evolved from these simple elements. As theater became more important as spectacle, the size of the altar diminished, the tithing house became the treasury, and the tiring house became the skene, the setting where the actors performed (as opposed to the orchestra, where only the chorus performed). The tiring house also served as the room from which the actors made their entrances and to which they retired.

Very little remains to us of the vast Athenian repertory of hundreds of plays, and most of the playwrights are known to us now only as names. But there is no doubt that the theater of Athens was a marvelously coordinated institution whose primary function was to celebrate Athenian culture, to teach morality, and to provide the citizenry with a sense of identity. In the Age of Pericles that institution was also to achieve artistic perfection, coming to rank alongside democracy, history, philosophy, and rhetoric as a major intellectual attainment.

For centuries most of what was known of Athenian theater came from Aristotle's *Poetics*. Although it was not composed until 344 B.C., eighty-five years after Pericles' death, it is the oldest and most complete account of Greek theater, its history, theory, and practice. Modern archaeology and scholarship have repeatedly questioned the authority of the *Poetics*, arguing that the work is late and that it is full of personal opinion and hearsay. However, it provides a wealth of information concerning the rules by which Greek playwrights composed their plays, a rationale for those rules, and even an account of their origin and history. Regardless of the rightness of Aristotle's sources and opinions—and disregarding the more serious question of how his work has been misinterpreted—the decisive effects that the *Poetics* have had on subsequent theater lore, criticism, and taste in Western Europe are enough to ensure it a place of importance in the history of the theater.

Athenian tragedy frequently celebrated the city-state's mythic past by presenting aspects of stories already well known to the spectators. In so doing, ancient Greek playwrights observed a uniform order of presentation, imposing rules of composition upon future playwrights and furnishing a familiar format by which the citizenry could judge the excellence of the works and their performance. Thus in theater, as in their strongly competitive public games, Athenians provided yet another dynamic assembly where the citizenry was involved in judging the worthiness of what their city government had chosen to sponsor.

The order of performance of a tragedy required that there be a prologue in which the playwright introduced the myth and the particular circumstances that he had chosen to present to the audience. Then followed the parodos, in which the chorus took possession of the orchestra, interposing itself between the audience and the action. Various episodes of the action were then presented, each linked to the other by the chants and dances of the chorus. The play ended with the exodos, during which the chanting chorus left the performing area.

The historic and social significance of the chorus, so often ignored in present-day productions of Greek tragedies, is a key to understanding the function of the theater in ancient Athens. The chorus, historically the oldest element in tragedy, is the conservative voice of the community against which the individual actions of the characters are to be judged. The chorus enters the theater before the announced action begins; it comments, sympathizes, and disagrees—and it admonishes the spectators between episodes—thus fixing the action of the play in a decidedly social context.

Instituted and supported by civil edict, the performance of plays was a principal part of the Dionysia, the celebrations by which Athens honored Dionysus, and attendance at the plays was mandatory for all citizens. A great vehicle in the form of a boat, commemorating Dionysus' mythic arrival from the sea, was drawn through the streets toward the sacred precinct below the Acropolis by performers disguised as satyrs. Atop the vehicle on a throne trimmed with vines, wearing the mask and garb of Dionysus, sat the chief player. In the performing area

The lighthearted vase painting below of helmeted warriors riding dolphins is thought to portray the semilegendary Greek dramatist Arion, who is said to have been rescued from drowning by a dolphin. It was Arion who first introduced an exchange of spoken lines between the Dionysian chorus and its leader. These declamations were designed to explain succeeding sections of the dithyramb, or hymn, to the audience. Other dramatists were to isolate the chorus leader as protagonist, then give him an antagonist.

of the sacred precinct, in view of all, stood an ancient wooden statue of the deity, a constant reminder that Dionysus was indeed the patron of this highly competitive set of ritual games.

Athenian audiences were avid and patient playgoers. Arriving at the theater at sunup, they customarily saw, in rapid succession, three plays by the same playwright on the same mythic action. These were followed by a fourth play, called the satyr play, in which the very myth that had just been performed with solemnity was broadly ridiculed—a healthy reaction, no doubt, to so much gravity.

Even if we grant the Athenians a longer attention span than our own, it is reasonable to conclude that the plays they saw were performed more rapidly than our own productions of Greek tragedies. The four plays must have finished at noon, for by early afternoon the bright Attic sun, which the audience had had at their backs all morning, would have been in their eyes—an ordeal in Athens, even in late March, when the Dionysia took place. Since breakfast was not a Greek custom, and the chestnuts, chickpeas, and broadbeans hawked in the stands were not substantial fare, the spectators left the shadeless area after the satyr play to eat their principal meal, ordinarily their only one, and to nap until late afternoon, when they returned to the theater to see a single comedy performed before dark.

The Dionysia, like the Christian Easter, was a celebration of resurrection, the most important feast of the liturgical year. Held at a time of the year when the Athenians were usually at home and not yet too busy with planting, commerce, or war, it was observed by everyone. Visitors came from Athens' distant colonies, and emissaries were sent

Linen or wooden masks enabled the principal actors of Greek drama to portray many roles in each production. Above is a sculptured stone version of the mask of tragedy. Two vases found in southern Italy evoke scenes from Euripides' Medea *and* The Trojan Women: *at left, Medea flees in a serpent-adorned chariot after murdering her children; below, Greeks prepare to sacrifice a Trojan girl.*

from tributary states with gifts for the Athenian treasury. Crowds of villagers swarmed to Athens, thronging the streets and filling the taverns and inns with their revelry. On the very first day of the six-day celebration, the new wine was broached, and the usually abstemious Athenians drank great quantities. Unlike the Lanaea, the feast that sponsored comedy, however, the Dionysia was celebrated with a certain degree of dignity; it was, after all, the chief feast of the city's most popular deity.

It has been estimated that the pre-Periclean theater, with its rude seating, could accommodate between 15,000 and 17,000 people, the less privileged spectators perching wherever they could. With such a crush, it is not surprising that the stands collapsed disastrously on at least two occasions, causing the city fathers to abandon the makeshift wooden bleachers for the stable stone seating arrangements we have come to associate with Greek theaters.

The permanent Theater of Dionysus was begun under Pericles about 435 B.C. and was finished seventy-five years later under Lycurgus. Although that structure was later replaced, it established the spatial relationships between the circular orchestra, where the chorus performed; the skene, the domain of the actors; and the theatai, where the audience sat. These basic relationships endured for almost six hundred years, and therefore the architectural modifications instituted by the later Greeks and Romans are clear indications of the changed attitudes toward the chorus, the actors, and even the theater itself. These changes, which took place gradually, can be quickly grasped by comparing the

great theater at Epidaurus, where the orchestra, skene, and theatai exemplify the accepted relationships of Pericles' time, with the ruins of the Theater of Dionysus in Athens, transformed by the Romans so that the skene cuts into the orchestra, and the orchestra itself is enclosed by a set of double walls that permit it to be flooded for aquatic spectacles. The chorus, once the most important element of Greek theater, had given way before the popularity of the actors, just as demands for spectacular entertainment of a definitely secular nature had enervated the purely sacred nature of the original rites.

It is one of history's enduring ironies that the great age of Greek theater passed before an adequate, unified building could be constructed to its specifications. Nevertheless, the Theater of Dionysus, begun under Pericles, was to become a model for theater building both in its own time and later throughout the Hellenistic world. It was at this same time that the various disparate elements that constitute Greek tragedy achieved an admirable interplay and balance. Those qualities are reflected in the physical plan of fourth-century Greek theaters, where the chorus, as commentator and civic conscience, was actually cut off from the actors by a high platform to which, in the early theater, there was no direct access. Even in later arrangements, when the chorus had lost its primary importance and the actor had become the center of attraction, the difference in levels was maintained, although access to the skene was made easier by a set of stairs. In the Periclean theater, the tiring house was brought alongside the orchestra and functioned both as an elaborate architectural frame against which the actors appeared and as an acoustical sounding-board. The spectators, once allowed to ring the entire orchestra, were now segregated from both actors and chorus by a wide passageway. They were further compelled to sit in the theatai, a steeply raked seating arrangement that

After watching three tragedies on an elevating theme, spectators at the Theater of Dionysus applauded as a horde of satyr players—decked out in horses' ears, tails, and phalluses—rushed onto the playing area and vented their energies upon such august personages as Hera (above, left) and Iris (above, right), who are shown in details from a kylix painting. After lunch and a nap, citizens gained readmittance to the afternoon's comedy with tokens of stone or ivory (below).

fanned out along slightly more than half the circumference of the orchestra.

The theatai itself was divided into wedge-shaped sections, each of which could be easily controlled by the officials who assigned the seats. The Athenians, for all their dignity, were an unruly audience, deeply imbued with a sense of competition and given to personal expression. They applauded loudly what they admired, but they stamped, shouted, and whistled when they found the presentation inferior. They were famous for generosity to winners, but they gave no quarter to losers. With such a responsive audience, it is no wonder that the city government exercised strong powers of censorship on playwrights, proscribing both acts of violence and provocative language in tragic plays. We can be quite sure that whatever the Greeks understood by catharsis, it was more rational than emotional, for Herodotus reports that the city fined the playwright Phrynichus a thousand drachmas for causing the audience to weep. It was even decreed that the offending play, *The Capture of Miletus*, should never again be presented.

Furthermore, seating was firmly regulated. Nearest the orchestra sat the priests of Dionysus, the city officials, and the choragus, the wealthy citizen who had, as a civic duty, paid for the production of the plays; with him sat the playwright, unless, as sometimes happened, he was taking part in the performance. Ranged just above the dignitaries and dressed in white sat the male citizenry of Athens. A special section was designated for the ephebi, eighteen-year-olds in combat training. Above them sat the women, and still higher those slaves whose masters had given them the day off. The villagers sat where they could. In Pericles' day the theater, like the courts of law, was understood to be a source of public instruction, so admission was free. Each spectator received a symbolon, a metal disc about the size of a large coin, upon which was inscribed the number of his seat. We do not know how the seats were allotted, but there must have been considerable haggling. Some seats bore official designations that can still be read, while some seats had unofficial graffiti, also still legible, scratched into them by spectators who wished thereby to claim the seats for their exclusive use.

It was the duty of the archon, or highest city official, to organize the competitions of tragic and comic plays for the Dionysia. From the plays submitted he personally selected the three tetralogies he deemed most worthy, assigning to each a choragus, or "angel," who paid for the entire production. From earliest times rich Athenians considered it a civic obligation to use their wealth to help glorify Athens, whether by building ships, equipping armies, providing buildings, or producing plays. It was, furthermore, considered a great honor to have produced a winning tetralogy.

For the Greeks of the fourth and fifth centuries B.C. the tragic tetralogies had a very special pertinence: they allowed for speculation on moral obligations. The Greeks watched the arguments in all these plays carefully, always considering the rightness or wrongness of

An open-mouthed, wide-eyed face of tragedy looks out from a fragment of fresco (left); the ivory statuette at right also wears a tragic mask. This statuette shows late Greek or early Roman costuming in the distorting height provided by its mask and by its stilted boots.

choices made by an individual with the same avid attention they gave to their many court suits. The problem would first be stated in abstract terms as a theme—after which the chorus, the official voice of society, would comment on it. The actor then presented the problem in more concrete terms, the chorus continuing to elucidate, admonish, judge, and pity. The plays were resolved in purely conventional—but always instructive—ways. Everything about them celebrated the unique way in which the Greeks had come to distinguish themselves from the rest of their neighbors: by weighing the rights of the individual against the rights of society and the claims of the gods.

Once Thespis had invented the tragic form by setting one member of the chorus apart from the others, thus creating the need for dialogue, it took only a century for tragedy to reach full development. The years of its greatness correspond closely to the combined lifetimes of Aeschylus, Sophocles, and Euripides, the master playwrights of Greece's golden age of theater. Of the hundreds of tragedies written by these three playwrights and their contemporaries, we possess only thirty-two. Seven of these are attributed to Aeschylus and seven to Sophocles; of the eighteen others, seventeen are undoubtedly the work of Euripides. Although they represent only a fraction of the whole, these thirty-two plays dramatically demonstrate the evolution of tragedy from a highly disciplined, authoritarian theater form to a celebration of the individual.

Scholars are not certain when Aeschylus was born, but it is known that he had established himself as a playwright by 500 B.C. Of his ninety tragedies, we know the names of seventy-nine. The handful that remain to us in actual text include the *Oresteia*, the only example we have of a complete trilogy. Aeschylus is thought to have fixed the order and form of tragedy, yet it seems likely that the order of prologue, chorus, report of the messenger, and final lament of the victims was already well established by the time the playwright added two more actors to the chorus. In his lifetime this form of high tragedy approached perfection, having developed from ritualistic beginnings—the various parts of which were not connected—to include those elements now recognized as the basic components of a play: action, conflict, characterization, and resolution. In reading the oldest of Aeschylus' plays, *The Persians*, we see just how deeply the Dionysia were committed to identifying and glorifying the civilization of Athens and the pride of its citizens.

In 468 B.C. Sophocles, who was almost thirty years younger than Aeschylus, won out over the older playwright at the Dionysia, thus marking the beginning of a long career that was to terminate only with his death in 406 B.C. Although the plays of Aeschylus are more powerful in scope, since they spring from vast, cosmic considerations and present characters of almost titanic proportion, the plays of Sophocles elicit our interest and sympathy because of the recognizable human qualities of his characters. Sophocles helped to secularize the spirit and content of tragedy by introducing a third actor and by reducing the role of the chorus—a tendency that grew, under his successors, to such a point that the chorus, already diminished to fifteen members from Aeschylus' original fifty, disappeared altogether. In keeping with a life-long devotion to physical beauty, Sophocles introduced realistically painted scenery to the theater, an innovation whose immediate acceptance indicates a significant step in the great changeover from an evocative theater to one of greater visual demands—demands that were to increase until the poetic reality of early Greek theater became confused with the reality of everyday life. That all these innovations were in the spirit of the times seems certain, for Sophocles' plays received both official and popular acclaim, won eighteen prizes, and led Aristotle to label his *Oedipus Rex* a model of excellence.

Euripides, only a little younger than Sophocles, was even more independent and individualistic in his outlook. His plays, full of skepticism, are outspoken and critical of established ways. In his lifetime he

won only five prizes, but his plays were better appreciated by later generations. Even today his plays are produced more often than those of either Aeschylus or Sophocles, probably because Euripides' interest in psychological complexities is similar to our own.

As we have already seen, the ancient Greeks were quick to punish levity and sacrilege with heavy fines or exile. But they understood that their institutions were man-made and that their government, staffed by men like themselves, was subject to the weaknesses of men. In short, they understood the folly of taking themselves too seriously. They knew and esteemed the therapeutic powers of laughter. Comedy had been with them even longer than tragedy, and as tragedy evolved, comedy also took its officially assigned place in the order of things. Indeed, each performance day of the Dionysia ended with the presentation of a comedy, allowing the spectators to end the day with laughter. These comedies used the same scenic arrangements as the tragic plays, often poking fun at the very machines that earlier in the day had lifted the gods in an apotheosis. And whereas the spectators sat at a decorous distance from the actors in the tragic plays, in comedy the actors often stepped forward and addressed individual officials in the crowd, calling attention to some political foible or misdeed. Pericles himself was not exempt from such public ridicule.

While comedies were presented during the Dionysia, the Lanaea was the true feast of comedy. Not many foreigners were likely to brave the rough December seas to attend these performances, so the Athenians could lambaste their officials unmercifully. This they did with such grotesque obscenities that no women were allowed to attend the presentations despite the fact that the Lanaea had from the earliest times been the official feast of women. The four great masters of Old Comedy were Crates, Cartinus, Eupolis, and Aristophanes, the last being the greatest comic genius and cleverest rascal of them all. So sharp were his eye and tongue that no public figure escaped censure in his plays. In spite of their love of satire, the Athenians detested unmitigated public ridicule, and as a result, Aristophanes was soundly beaten on several occasions for his candor.

Long after the decline of Greek tragedy, comedy continued to reign supreme, but after Aristophanes' death only one playwright, Menander, distinguished himself sufficiently to be remembered. His plays are entirely different from the rough-and-tumble political satires of Aristophanes, being amusing, often pleasantly bawdy pieces whose main source of fun lies in their complicated plot structure. Menander invented the clever slave, who was to become a stock character in European theater literature. He was also the only one of ancient Athens' great playwrights to see the theater building begun under Pericles' administration finished and inaugurated.

In the earliest celebrations of tragedy, the actor was something of a priest. He was deputized by the officials to play in "place of the people," just as the athlete was chosen to compete in "place of the people" and to represent them at the games. This distinction is helpful in explaining the nature and function of the actor in what Jacob Burkhardt called the "agonal," or competitive, element of Greek culture. To the Greeks, who organized every aspect of their personal and cultural life along competitive lines, both the games and the tragic plays were serious competitions; for them the word "sport" had none of the trivial connotations that it possesses for us. Not only were tragic plays produced for an official competition; their very composition, pitting the individual against the elements—against fate, against society and other individuals—depended upon competition, and it was the force of this basic and pervasive struggle that gave vigor to every line of dialogue.

Actors, like athletes, had to train—and while the ancient theaters were famous for their extraordinary acoustics, the actor's voice had to be strong, agile, and melifluous to be heard and accepted by critical Athenian audiences. The actor wore high boots with thick platform soles, a conventional robe, and a large mask surmounted by an elaborately coifed wig. He was literally hidden within an effigy, which it was his task to animate, moving atop his stilt-like boots with the grace of a dancer, and speaking through the mask with force and artistry so that every word reached the last ranks of his audience of 15,000.

The appointed sponsor paid for the masks and costumes of the chorus members. He also provided food for the entire cast during rehearsals and paid each cast member according to contract. The actor had to provide his own costumes and masks, however. The latter were fashioned of wood, leather, or stiffened linen, and the best were treasured not only because they were expensive but because through long use they had become extremely comfortable to wear. The actor kept

The grin that dominates the mask of the declaiming actor above identifies him as a comedian, and the well-padded bodies and pendulous phalluses of the players on the vase at left mark them for similar roles. Adopting the costumes of Greek Old Comedy, these Roman farceurs play out a scene depicting the birth of Helen in which Hephaestus tries to cleave the egg from which Helen rises.

Overleaf: *In a mosaic from Pompeii, actors dress for a play.*

24

his masks in excellent repair, seeing to it that they were freshly painted for each engagement. The costumes and hand properties were all conventionally designed, permitting the spectators to readily identify the characters as they appeared, and later plays were constructed so that an actor could play two roles with enough time allowed between exits and entrances for a change of costume and mask. (To enter the playing area without a mask was considered highly inappropriate, even in comedy productions. On the rare occasions in which comedians appeared without masks, they therefore painted their faces to obscure their real identity.) Only men could appear on the Athenian stage, and a good playwright would often write in such a way that the main actor could demonstrate the range of his talents by playing first a man's role and then a woman's.

Tragic actors in ancient times were respected citizens, and the more gifted ones were in great demand, being paid handsomely to travel to distant places for festival appearances. On the other hand, because the satirical and political nature of Old Comedy was local, there was little demand for comedians out of their own region. As a result, comic acting as a profession did not develop until Menander had changed the composition of comedy to answer more universal, apolitical demands.

In the Pompeiian mosaic opposite, two male actors play the parts of women consulting a sorceress—a role likewise played by a male. In the fresco at right a Roman actor has removed his tragic mask, which is being admired by a female fan.

Long before there was such a thing as an actor, however, itinerant mimes, unimpeded by language barriers, were plying their trade throughout the known world—in market places, army camps, palaces, and village clearings. Since the nature of his art is allied to satire, the mime chooses his materials from the commonplaces of ordinary experience, pointing out human foibles and weaknesses. He is a kind of conjurer who gives the spectator the impression of seeing what is not really there, creating through disciplined gestures imaginary objects whose existence he then sustains through his own concentrated observance of them. By changing his physical appearance in a flash, he transforms himself into another person, an animal, or an object—his success depending upon his virtuosity and quickness. In 430 B.C. Sophron wrote a mime play, thus elevating this folk art to a literary form. There followed a brilliant period for mime, one that lasted right into the Dark Ages following the fall of Rome. In the interval, the mime became a celebrity whose entr'acte appearance was soon as necessary to Attic theater as clown acts are to circuses. The great mimes of Hellenistic times grew wealthy and influential, yet something of their disreputable origin always remained with them.

The Romans, great admirers of the Greeks, instituted their own "stage games" as early as 364 B.C. But the cultural significance that had, so to speak, monitored the evolution of Athenian theater was lacking in Rome. Instead, the Romans saw a pragmatic and political aspect of theater that would have shocked the Athenians. For the Romans, theater was a convenient meeting place for entertainment and ostentation. Consequently, the early wooden structures modeled on the fifth-cen-

The Pompeiian fresco at left has preserved a scene from one of the comedies of Plautus in which two women listen to the talk of a slave; the Pompeiian painting at right depicts a theatrical scene, complete with velarium—a hanging that eventually evolved into the stage curtain—at top. Above is a second-century comic mask.

tury Greek ones were soon abandoned for large, imposing stone buildings erected as monuments to the republic. (The Romans also favored realistically painted scenery; indeed, the oldest extant treatise on scenography was written by the Roman Vitruvius about 100 B.C.) These spacious new theater buildings were excellent places for assembling the populace, and Roman officials were quick to see their political possibilities, decreeing that towns throughout the empire should include a theater in their municipal planning. With the creation of this chain of theaters, Roman actors were assured of a good living if they chose to tour the provinces, and many of them did.

Roman playwrights never achieved anything like the eminence of their Greek predecessors, but two writers of comedy deserve mention: Plautus, who had been a mime in his youth; and Terence, a Carthaginian Berber who had come to Rome as a slave. Both worked in the direction Menander had indicated, developing the situation comedy of cross plots and mistaken identities. They also created a collection of stock characters who were to take up permanent residence in European literature, among them Maccus, the wily slave; miles gloriosus, the braggart soldier; and innumerable victims of mistaken identity. Both Terence and Plautus were major influences on such Renaissance writers as Shakespeare, Tirso de Molina, and Lope de Vega.

Both Plautus and Terence were soon forgotten, however, as the Romans abandoned plays for spectacles of more sensational interest.

Masked actors represented in the mosaic at left play their instruments for Roman spectators. Under the Romans, Greek tragedy and comedy were gradually debased and replaced by public spectacles; eventually, plays were abandoned altogether, arenas were filled with water, and mock naval battles were staged. Somewhat later, beasts or men were pitted against men, as depicted in the second-century mosaics opposite, which feature gladiatorial combat.

The Colosseum, finished in A.D. 80, could seat 50,000 spectators, far too great a number to be entertained by the intimate intricacies of plays. At popular insistence, the classic actor disappeared—to be replaced, in rapid succession, by comic sketches, mime shows, clown acts, acrobatic displays, and rope dancing. These in turn gave way to aquatic displays, for which the arena was flooded. Animal baiting became popular, and finally human combat caught the fleeting interest of the Roman crowd. The age of classic theater was finished, and a set of attitudes toward the role of theater in society had disappeared.

2

Mystery, Miracle, Magic, and Mime

NOTHING BETTER ILLUSTRATES the disintegration of the classic Athenian theater than the disappearance of the satyr play and the substitution of the mime play after the featured tragedy. The intention of the early satyr plays had been corrective; behind their aura of ridicule lay a deep and abiding moral concern. The intention of the mime plays, on the other hand, was burlesque—an effort to domesticate the myths and destroy their power. It was, therefore, almost inevitable that in the atmosphere of permissiveness and secularization that characterized Hellenistic times —from roughly the fourth to the first century B.C.—mime should flourish. Because mime performances were short, brilliant, and obscene—and because they always dealt with easily recognizable material—they were enthusiastically received by the public. The classic actor had felt honored when he was awarded the palm as a prize in dramatic competition. Not so the mime: he demanded gold in payment for his performance—and he got it. The most successful mimes quickly grew wealthy, and often came to be politically influential as well. It was as mimes, incidentally, that the first actresses dared to appear on the stage.

As we have seen, the art of the mime was chiefly one of caricature. It demanded a quick eye for detail and a gift for ironic insight, as well as the skill to translate both into an easily understood play of gestures. Moreover, it was by long tradition anti-authoritarian and irreverent. The mime play provoked ready laughter from the audience, but it was often as unpleasant as a bee sting to its victim, and as a result mimes were constantly falling in and out of favor. No sooner had the Christian Church begun to impose its authority on imperial Rome, for example, than it recognized the mime as an antagonist. Tertulian, Origen, John Chrysostom, and many other fathers of the Church repeatedly denounced mimes as obscene servants of the devil—and the mimes retaliated by presenting caricatures of self-righteous clerics in their performances. The Church in its turn put all performers under general interdiction, banning classic actors, mimes, buffoons, jugglers, and acrobats indiscriminately, refusing them the Sacraments and excluding them from the Christian community.

Thus banished, the mimes reverted to their ancient ways and became vagabonds, playing to whomever would come out to watch them. They literally formed "motley crews," dressing outrageously to attract attention. Outlawed and forced by Church ban to fraternize

When the doublet-clad actor seen in this medieval manuscript illustration painted by Renaud de Montauban has added the horned mask to his costume, he will be ready to act the role of the devil in a Mystery play.

with criminals in an underground society, mimes acquired a shady reputation that stuck with them right up to the present century—and tainted all professional actors by association. But to judge from the increasingly vituperative quality of the Church decrees and the harshness of the punishment meted out, the mimes did not stop performing. On the contrary, they must have specialized in anticlerical pieces, for one of the decrees threatens "corporal punishment and banishment . . . if any actor . . . put on garment belonging to priestly rank, or a monk's dress or a nun's dress or any ecclesiastic . . ."

The mimes took underground with them all the theater lore and skills of the Roman stage. They became, in effect, the guardians of all the stock characters that Plautus and Terence had created: the wily slave, the miser, the charlatan, the braggart soldier, the litigious scholar. Forced together by circumstance, mimes, actors, dancers, acrobats, rope dancers, and musicians joined forces to survive. In an atmosphere where performers fashioned presentations from their combined skills, recalling what they could of ancient texts (which they modified to suit the needs of the moment), the distinctive type of theater that was later called commedia dell'arte was born. Making use of the stock characters lifted wholesale from the works of Plautus and Terence, performers soon dispensed with trying to recall the texts, substituted stock situations from which they improvised, and extended the dialogue with songs, dances, and acrobatic stunts.

The natural roots of theater are nourished by man's urge to imitate, to play, to embellish the ordinary. These impulses refuse to be frus-

Below, sixteenth-century actors dressed as animals, jesters, and devils begin to debark from a "ship of fools" being wheeled into the center of Nuremberg to break the melancholy spell of Lent. Annual reenactments of Jesus of Nazareth's birth, agony, and resurrection were an important part of medieval dramatic fare, as were dramatizations of the miracles of saints. Accounts of the miracles wrought by the Virgin are told in the Cantigas de Santa Maria *and illustrated in the manner shown at right.*

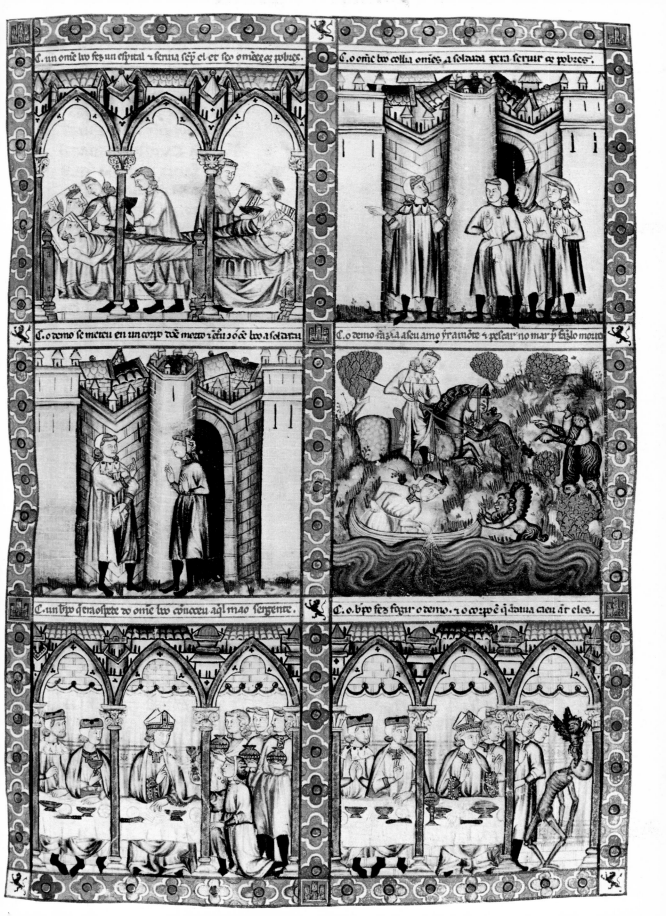

C. un ome bo fez un espital ꝛ seruia seṗ el ꝛ seꝯ omēꝯ oꝯ pobꝛeſ.

C. o ome bo colla omieſ ꞇa solaꝛa ṗꝛa ſeruir oꝯ pobꝛeſ.

C. o ꝺemo ſe meteu en un coꝛpo ꝺꝛ meꝛꞇu ꝛ oꝯ oe bo a solaꝛꞇu

C. o ꝺemo faɀia aſeu amo Ꟊꞇa mꝺꞇe ꝛ peſcar no mar ṗ tablo mouꞇ

C. un bꝓ q̓ eꝛa oſpeꝺe ꝺo omē bo cōneceu aql mao ſerꟉente.

C. o bꝓ fez foɀir o ꝺemo ꝛ o coꝛꝑē q̓ ꝺꞇua eꞇeu aꞇ eleſ.

· · · · · · · · ·

didera S eculorum amen l nmandauf t iafion Cuf

· · · · · · · ·

rodadnf S eculo rum amen R ubrum S caf de cur fuf

· · · · · · · Iõ.v.

S eculorum amen R cccuf de ca t xpugna PLAGITRIT

N oeo eane

G loriapatri & filio

& fpir tuf fancto Sicut

erat inprincipio &

nunc & fem per &

infecula feculof

Amen —— Circum

trated indefinitely; when they are forbidden expression in one area, they find another. And thus when the Church proscribed secular theater, another form of dramatic expression sprang up within the Church itself. The Christian liturgical calendar is divided into major and minor feasts. Easter and Christmas, the greatest of the major celebrations, are preceded respectively by Lent and Advent, periods of penitential preparation, observed in medieval times with strict fasts and abstinence from meat. During both Lent and Advent, brightly colored vestments, flowers, and the usual number of lamps and candles were forbidden in the celebration of the Mass. With the arrival of Christmas or Easter, however, the altar was decorated with flowers, banks of candles and lamps were lit, and gold vestments were prescribed. This dramatic change fostered other embellishments: on Christmas Eve, for example, a manger scene was set up near the main altar, with beautifully dressed dolls representing the Blessed Virgin, Saint Joseph, the angels, and the shepherds. On the stroke of midnight, the image of the Infant Jesus was paraded in solemn procession and installed in the manger, around which a ceremony of carols was performed.

On Easter Sunday, a trope, or dramatic commentary, was performed in which a white-clad priest, representing the angel at the tomb, sat in one corner of the church, and three others, dressed as the Three Marys, approached him. The following lines were chanted:

> *Quem quaeritis in sepulchro, O Christicolae?*
> *Jesum Nazarenum crucifixum, O Coelicolae.*
> *Non est hic: surrexit sicut praedixerat.*
> *Ite, nuntiate quia surrexit de sepulchro.*

("Whom seek ye in the tomb, O followers of Christ? The crucified Jesus of Nazareth, O ministers of Heaven. He is not here: He has risen as he predicted. Go, announce that He has risen from the tomb.")

The admixture of secular and sacred elements marks much of the history of drama. Jesters, such as the dancer decorating the Latin manuscript at left, represent a ubiquitous secular tradition, but the platform furnishings below, built by the city of Valenciennes for its passion play in 1547, are distinctly sacred. They include, from the left: Paradise, Nazareth, the Temple, Jerusalem, a palace, a golden door, the sea, and hell's mouth.

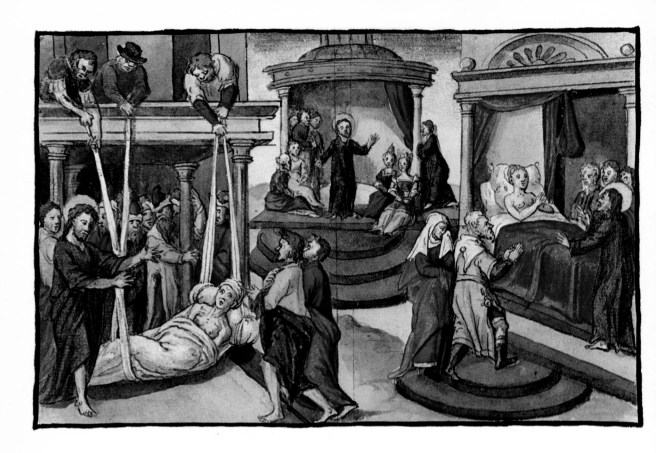

This little four-line dialogue, dating from A.D. 969, is thought to be the beginning of medieval drama, a distinct form that owes nothing to the theaters of Greece or Rome. While the trope goes back to the Greeks, who used it to explain a point by inserting a commentary in the text, this peculiar medieval use of it as a dramatic extension of the text itself is significant, since it marks with historical accuracy the beginning of a characteristic development in European theater: the formal use, in specific situations, of the lazzo, which the performer improvised extensively, using the text as a mere framework.

The use of tropes in dramatic dialogue during the celebration of Mass and the recitation of the canonical hours won widespread approval in medieval Europe. As a result, tropes were introduced so generously into the Christmas and Easter services that they soon vied with the Mass and the Holy Office for attention and had to be detached from the ceremonies. These systems of embellishments, organized around major feasts, were the nucleus of the great religious-play cycles. The Church, bound to expurgate the ceremonies yet eager to keep the plays under close surveillance, ordered them out of the churches but allowed them to be played on the porches or the front steps of those buildings. With the plays transferred to these locations, the Church for some time continued as producer and chief sponsor.

The religious plays were of two general types: Mystery plays, which dramatized theological mysteries such as the Incarnation and of which the Wakefield Cycle is a splendid example—and the Miracle plays, which reenacted miraculous happenings attributed to saints or to holy relics. At one time or another every cathedral town in Christen-

In a scene from the renowned Valenciennes passion play (left, above), three episodes from the life of Jesus are shown simultaneously: the lowering of the palsied man, Jesus' conversion of Mary Magdalene, and his resurrection of a girl. The gamboling jester at right—this time a bronze statue from Germany—was occasionally incorporated into Miracle and Mystery plays.

Overleaf: After he had viewed the scene in Mystery plays, Hans Schäufelein painted this picture of the manacled Jesus being presented to the people.

dom supported a troupe of players and technicians whose job it was to see that the local play cycle was performed at an appointed time in the liturgical year. The players were amateurs selected from both the clergy and laity, and the popular success of these productions was so overwhelming that pageant wagons were often built at great expense so that the plays might be taken on tour.

Moving the plays outside the church building proved to be more than a simple exercise in logistics—it was also a definite step toward secularization. As in the case of the Greek theater, the shift from the imaginary setting that myth and ritual require to the realistic setting and lifelike detail that ordinary imaginations seem to demand brought about the secularization of these religious plays. Almost at once they moved down into the marketplace. There elaborate settings, called mansions, were built for the staging of each of the episodes, the final

Medieval manuscript illustrations provide us with pictures of countless singers and storytellers. In a miniature from the Roman de la Rose *(above), itinerant entertainers amuse themselves in a garden; below, masked musicians and comedians perform in a detail from the manuscript of the* Roman de Fauvel. *Opposite, a troubadour in his familiar pointed shoes is posed within a fourteenth-century landscape in an illustration from the* Livre des cent ballades.

one being a "hell mouth" that spat real smoke and flames in scenes depicting the Last Judgment. Sometimes the spectators moved from mansion to mansion—a custom still seen in certain churches at the celebration of the Stations of the Cross. When the crowds were too great for such an orderly arrangement, bleachers were set up for them.

As was natural, long-censured professional performers gradually began to infiltrate these amateur productions. No doubt the performances grew better as a result, but renewed interdictions followed. The Church forbade all clerics to perform, and it withdrew its patronage from the spectacles, designating them as occasions of sin.

Thus by the end of the thirteenth century, the status of the professional performer in Europe was still that of an outlaw who won favor from time to time yet had no recognized place in society and consequently no rights to property. Forced to wander from place to place, he earned his keep by his wits and by his ability to please, amuse, and answer the whims of his host. Some of these performers wandered about on their own as troubadours, performing wherever they could for whatever host would take them in for the night. More often, for safety's sake, actors banded together. As a troupe they could attract more spectators, and if they were forbidden to play in the marketplace, their encampment made a suitable enough place to perform. Like the early Greek comedians whose name they commemorated, they too were condemned to wander from village to village in disrepute.

fima parte gravemente sono e poi si
meno elqual men grave sono e spresso
mexon edisopa mexon diceumenon
nelultima esupremo parte deltecorto
sono ypoleon voce sottilissime edacu
tissime dipoi nelmezo deltecorto ein
tro lelinie delle circumferentie alspo
to refereischi diceinando delcirculo in
elcantro lasciena chossuo pulpito nesia

voci Ineg[r]odi

hooreffestea

tecorto

3

Comedy at Court,
Comics in the Streets

*The Sienese artist and architect
Francesco di Giorgio, a poly-
math noted for his military con-
structions, also contributed a
number of civilian structures to
his home town, among them the
cathedral of Siena. Di Giorgio's
sketch of a typical fifteenth-century theater reveals the persistent
influence of Roman forms upon
early Renaissance architects.*

IN 1438 THE BYZANTINE EMPEROR John Paleologus led an embassy to
Florence to beg the mighty house of Medici for help in defending his
capital, Constantinople, against the Ottoman Turks. In the emperor's
company were a number of scholars who so impressed Cosimo de' Medici
with their knowledge of the ancient Greeks that he established an
academy to encourage the study of Greek texts in Florence. Fifteen years
later, when Constantinople fell to the Turks, thousands of refugees flooded into Italy through Venice. Among them were two groups of people
who were to have a deep influence upon the growth of theater in
Europe: scholars and mimes. Byzantine scholars brought with them a
wealth of ancient Greek manuscripts—and the learning to interpret
them. As a result they were quickly welcomed into the Florentine
Academy, and into the similar centers that other townships set up,
based upon the Medici model. The mimes, for their part, brought to
Italy a thousand-year-old tradition of improvisation—and the ability to
adapt it to local usage. The arrival of these refugees in Europe marks
the beginning of two forms of theater: the commedia erudita, a literary
theater based on ancient texts, and the commedia dell'arte, a theater of
virtuosity based on improvisation. Both forms were to dominate European theater for more than four centuries.

Yet the arrival of these refugees from Byzantium does not in itself
explain the immediate interest they inspired and the widespread acceptance accorded them. Among other things, Latin, not Greek, had been
the lingua franca of European scholars for several centuries—the final
schism between the Eastern and Western Churches in the eleventh century having dramatically reduced the opportunities for Western scholars to study Greek. Then, following the fall of Constantinople, the
sudden influx of Greek scholars and manuscripts made it possible for
Europeans to learn Greek and to familiarize themselves with many
aspects of the ancient past of which they had previously been ignorant.
Greek became the new language of scholars, and the study of Greek
manuscripts became the vogue in every center of learning in Europe.

During these years the refugee scholars of Byzantium, much in
demand, traveled widely, sowing the seeds of Greek humanism and Platonic philosophy. Never before had there been such an interest in the
past. Princes and prelates became amateur antiquarians. Bankers, who
had never before bothered with such matters, interested themselves in

literary sidelines and even financed archaeological excavations, displaying the unearthed objects in their living quarters, gardens, and studies. Wealthy merchants, having learned to read Latin and Greek, collected books and curiosities from the past, their private collections forming the beginnings of the great libraries and museums of Europe.

But humanist studies of antiquity did not necessarily yield an accurate impression of Greek and Latin philosophy and culture. To the scholars of the fifteenth and sixteenth centuries, the ancient past was a dream world inhabited by beautiful nymphs and shepherds, gods and goddesses. This idyllic state, called Arcadia or Utopia, was assigned to a vague geographic location in ancient Greece; its chronology, equally vague, bore the designation of the "Golden Age." All these notions plainly derived from the humanists' understanding of Plato's teaching about a pre-existing world of ideas. The humanists were further convinced that the ancients had known the answers to all the problems that beset mankind, and they believed that a thorough study of the remains of the past would reveal the answers.

This strongly Platonic persuasion gave an idealistic rather than a realistic bias to the humanists' studies. Where theater was concerned, for example, it caused them to misconstrue the plays of Plautus, Terence, and Seneca. Ignorant as they were of the painted exuberance of ancient Greece and Rome, the humanists projected an ordered, white, intellectual world from the sun-bleached remains they studied. Such mistaken speculation gave rise to an ideal aesthetics and poetics—from which canons of taste the humanists composed commedia erudita, learned, intellectual plays that they were fond of staging for each other in their academies and private gatherings.

But these productions were little more than staged readings. Since fifteenth-century humanists possessed no information about ancient acting styles, they based their ideas of delivery on Cicero's rules of

The ancient Romans' love of spectacle survived the empire's fall by many centuries, as the panoramic view below indicates. Painted on a trousseau chest by a sixteenth-century Florentine artist, it depicts the bridal procession of a daughter of the Adimari family. During this period Roman-style theaters reappeared. The first of these was the famed Teatro Olimpico in Vincenza (right), begun by the renowned architect Andrea Palladio according to Vitruvius' classical work on architecture.

rhetoric. It was not until the sixteenth century, when Aristotle's *Poetics* had become widely known, that Renaissance playwrights learned that ancient Greek drama was primarily concerned with action, which was distinct from rhetoric, the art of persuasion through words alone. The discovery in 1486 of Vitruvius' *Ten Books of Architecture* must have been another shock for the idealists. Vitruvius' fifth book gives a detailed account of the flamboyant technology of the late Hellenistic theaters, one that the humanists mistakenly accepted as a general description of Greek stagecraft in the fifth century B.C. This mistake was to persist for generations, and thus, a century later, the architect Palladio was commissioned to construct a theater in Vicenza according to Vitruvius' specifications. Completed by Palladio's successor, Scamozzi, this theater was inaugurated in 1584 with a performance of

Sophocles' *Oedipus Rex*. It is the most splendid example we have of a Renaissance theater building. Along with the Farnese Theater in Parma, another magnificent house, it gives us a fine idea of the Italian *teatro stabile*, the forerunner of the European opera house of a century and a half later.

Like the Hellenistic Greeks and the late Romans, Renaissance Italians, contrary to their sober philosophical aspirations, loved spectacle and indulged their fondness for civic pomp and display on every occasion. State visits, royal progresses, and the betrothals, marriages, baptisms, and funerals of important citizens were celebrated with great splendor and virtuosity. Wealthy burghers and civic officials turned to such artists as Leonardo da Vinci, Raphael, and Michelangelo, inviting them to create fantastic pageant floats and firework displays in which all manner of subjects from Greek mythology were realized with astonishing ingenuity.

As could be expected, these marvels soon found their way into the theater. Following what he believed were the indications of Vitruvius, Sebastiano Serlio created an archetypal setting for tragedy, comedy, and satire using the newly discovered laws of heightened perspective. In 1563 he published reproductions of these settings along with a treatise and explanations. Thus began an era of unparalleled richness in theater design and scenography that was to last for more than two hundred years, largely due to the remarkably prolonged activities of the great Bibiena family of theater designers.

While Byzantine scholars and their treasury of ancient manuscripts were helping to create the literary theater of the commedia erudita, with its stabilizing architecture and scenography, Byzantine mimes were busy accommodating their improvisatory skills to the Italian tradition of popular theater. Whereas the nobility, the rich merchant class, and the scholars favored an intellectual theater with voguish philosophical implications, ordinary folk favored the theater of the street and marketplace. As with the earlier theater of the medieval mimes, there was nothing stable about this popular form—no literary conventions, not even a proper script. There was no theater building, only a stage improvised from market trestles and wagon sheets that could be set up or struck in a flash. There were no tickets, just free-will offerings from the crowd. Yet these very unstable conditions demanded a specific excellence in performance. Contrary to the commedia erudita, whose

The patronage of the Medici family underwrote much of the Renaissance glory of Florence and helped support the new fashion in France as well. In the tapestry at left, Catherine de Médicis and her husband, Henry II of France, are being entertained at an elaborate outdoor pageant complete with a sea monster. An anonymous artist recorded the highly theatrical coronation of a poet in an Arcadian setting (right).

audiences were closed gatherings of intellectuals, the popular theater played to a disorderly crowd that was free to come and go, to be attentive or truculent—and that demanded to be constantly entertained.

The style of these popular performances was broad, hair-trigger quick in improvisation, and sensitively cued to the slightest whim of the spectators. It was called commedia dell'arte, a term that may be unclear to us today but was quite clear to the Italians of the Renaissance—to whom it meant a theater of astonishing virtuosity in performing skills. If the playwright was king in the commedia erudita, the actor ruled supreme in the commedia dell'arte. For this theater of skills, an actor had to possess not only the usual training in voice, movement, and impersonation; he also had to be skilled in music, dance, mime, fencing, juggling, prestidigitation, and rope dancing.

The traditional commedia dell'arte troupe consisted of at least eight players. Unlike our contemporary actors, whose skill is so often measured by their ability to play many characters convincingly, a comedian of that era specialized in one well-defined character, whom he played from the beginning to the end of a long career. Abiding by the classic practice of improvising within a strictly imposed frame of reference, the commedia dell'arte actor, while sticking religiously to his one easily recognized character, embellished outrageously.

Most of the major characters in these plays were of equal importance. They were types drawn from the Italian household, with its well-established system of responsibilities to honor, its dowries to haggle over, its lackeys and servants to control, its innkeepers to intrigue with. Most of the plots concern two or more households. At the head of each is a stock character. Pantalone, for instance, is an old, respected *magnifico*, the original merchant of Venice. He wears the scarlet suit of the well-heeled Venetian burgher, with its old-fashioned tie-hitched breeches and codpiece, from which dangles a lawn handkerchief. Over his shoulders he wears a narrow black cape, and on his head a little black cap. His half-mask gives him a hooked nose and moles, and his goatee accentuates the thrust of his chin. On one side of his waist he carries a pouch for money and papers, on the other a dirk. He is the head of a family, and he usually has a marriageable daughter.

The two wood engravings at left, from an illustrated edition of the comedies of Terence published in Lyon in 1493, include stage directions. In the print at near left, the character wearing striped pants appears twice, indicating the direction that the actor playing his role is to take. In the sixteenth-century work below, stock commedia dell'arte characters are presented by an artist of the Venetian school.

Graziano is the head of another family. He is a doctor of laws from Bologna, so he wears a great black cloak, beaver hat, and spectacles. His bulbous nose and bushy eyebrows are black with ink stains. He always carries books or manuscripts, sometimes both, and he frequently uses these to bolster his legal arguments. He and Pantalone have been friends since student days, but they often indulge in violent and protracted arguments. Graziano often has a son who is interested in marrying Pantalone's daughter, and consequently the arguments about dowries and property rights are endless.

There is always a captain in the troupe, a direct descendant of the miles gloriosus of late Roman comedy and the predecessor of Sir John Falstaff. This captain is a poppinjay in high leather boots and a leather doublet. His moustache is almost as large as the plume in his hat, and the sword he carries at his side is ancient and badly nicked. He is penniless, a liar and a coward who is forever boasting of past exploits in his native Spain.

Arlecchino, sometimes called Truffaldino, is the wily servant. He is from Bergamo, a mountainous region that furnished Venice with servants, and he is always hungry. He wears a loosely fitting suit of many patches and a little hat trimmed with a rabbit scut. Attached to his loose black belt is a small pouch containing a staggering number of worthless bits of pocket trash—pieces of bread, string, torn handkerchiefs—and stuck into the belt, like a sword, is a wooden slapstick. Arlecchino wears a dark half-mask with a large mole on the forehead. He is usually accompanied by several zanni, the old designation for

unskilled laborers. The wily servant usually manages to trick these poor fellows into doing his work by promising them things that he cannot supply once the work is accomplished, and thus the cunning little man from Bergamo must elude the duped zanni at the play's end.

With such a collection of characters confronting one another, commedia dell'arte plays simply happened. They were not written down except as abstracts that gave only the briefest sketch of the plot—and never the dialogue. It was up to the company manager to choose the situations, and it was he who posted the scenario minutes before the actors went on. These scenarios could be changed in a moment, without notice, to suit the demands of the audience, so that the abstract was only a pretext for the lazzi, or specialties of the various actors. These lazzi were either verbal or gestural. When one was particularly successful, it was often incorporated into the scenario and became, with repetition, a standard feature. Every actor had his bag of personalized tricks. One famous Pantalone, for example, is reported to have been able to punctuate his long speeches with a cartwheel until he was more than eighty years old.

The fame of the Italian commedia dell'arte troupes spread throughout Europe in the fourteenth, fifteenth, and sixteenth centuries. Large communities of Italians were living abroad during those years, and

Cap. Babeo   Cucuba

In the mobile street productions that were commedia dell'arte, an actor adopted for life the role of a stock character. Above, from the left: the distaff half of a pair of lovers; the doltish, crook-nosed servant who evolved into Pagliacci, Pierrot, and Punch; the flamboyant but cowardly captain later familiar as Falstaff; and another view of the agile and skilled servant Arlecchino.

Overleaf: *Masters join their coachmen's argument in a famous commedia dell'arte scene.*

roving troupes were invited to play for them. (The first such invitation was extended by the large community of Italians connected with the silk industry in Lyon.) Catherine de Médicis took a commedia dell'arte troupe to Paris with her when she became queen of France, and those players quickly became the darlings of the court. Molière, over a long period of time, shared his theater with a commedia dell'arte troupe, sometimes taking a role in their productions. What he learned of their distinctive style and their love for introducing "bits" and intermezzi into the structure of a play can be seen in many of his own works.

As their fame grew, these skilled Italians were offered every inducement to travel to other countries. They went to Munich, to Linz, and eventually to Copenhagen, where a love for Italian comedy has remained to this day (the world's oldest commedia-style troupe still performs in the Tivoli Gardens). They also went to England, where, judging from many allusions in his plays, Shakespeare himself saw them. Everywhere they were received with enthusiasm, a strong indication that it was indeed their remarkable skills at mime, dancing, and improvisation, rather than their use of dialogue, that distinguished commedia dell'arte players from any others, making them equally understandable in all foreign countries.

The Italian troupes continued to earn their fortunes abroad until

late in the eighteenth century. Aware by then that the style was dying, the Venetian playwright Count Carlo Gozzi tried to prolong its life by writing fantasies, hoping that the late-eighteenth-century love of make-believe and magic might draw more people to the theater, where his scenarios would provide the actors with an opportunity to use their skills to advantage. But the great age of commedia dell'arte had passed. Goldoni, another talented Venetian of this period, finding the commedia dell'arte inferior to the refined comedies of Molière, wrote literary plays for the Italian companies in which the stock characters were still employed. Yet for all their charm, Goldoni's plays lack that bravura and crudity that had given commedia dell'arte its distinctive style. Refinement proved disastrous for the ancient theatrical form, and by the beginning of the nineteenth century, the once supremely popular commedia style had fallen entirely out of favor. There have been attempts to recreate it in recent years, but even those brilliant productions have only served to demonstrate that commedia dell'arte is of another time, and responds to another set of theatrical demands.

4

The Golden Age
of European Drama

London's lords and coachmen, ladies and merchants, applauded the action of Shakespeare's history plays, awaited the inescapable fates of his tragic characters, and entered the realm of fantasy through the lyricism of his romantic comedies—as did the painter J. H. Füssli in his evocation of A Midsummer Night's Dream. *In this detail an enchanted Titania embraces Bottom despite his donkey's head.*

WHILE THE ITALIANS were creating a new poetics, architecture, and scenography for their theater—and in the commedia dell'arte troupes, a new structure for professional acting companies—the rest of Western Europe was following the long-established theatrical conventions of the Morality, Miracle, and Cycle plays. Thanks to the efforts of such traveling humanists as Erasmus, however, the new Italian aesthetic quickly spread to university circles throughout Spain, France, the Low Countries, and England. Everywhere that the new teaching was introduced an immediate interest in literary theater sprang up. Spanish, French, Dutch, and English schoolmen, emulating their Italian counterparts, wrote new plays using Plautus, Terence, and Seneca as models. Around 1553, for example, an English scholar named Nicholas Udall wrote *Ralph Roister Doister*, the first comedy in English. Ten years later two of Udall's contemporaries, Thomas Sackville and Thomas Norton, wrote the first English tragedy, *Gorboduc*, which was based, inevitably, upon Seneca, and which was performed for Queen Elizabeth upon one of her visits to the Inner Temple.

As the vogue for mythological pageantry replaced medieval Church plays and the "Italianate gentleman" became the accepted model for personal behavior, Italian scholars, painters, architects, musicians, tailors, and dancing masters flocked to the courts of Spain, France, and England. Those who could traveled to Italy to see for themselves the marvels that the new humanism had created in Venice, Ferrara, and Florence; returning home, they exercised the prerogatives of connoisseurs, distaining crude native arts. Indeed, the prestige of things Italian was so great that some conservative schoolmen feared that the English would lose their national identity. The Italian phrase *Inglese italianato é un diabolo incarnato*—"an Italianized Englishman is a living devil"—went the rounds.

English courtiers were quick to imitate the elaborate spectacles they had witnessed in Italy. Especially favored were the intermezzi, which were designed to be played between the courses of state banquets. The English were notoriously stalwart trenchermen; they demanded three heavy meals a day and expected to be regaled at banquets with three or four dishes at each course. Small wonder, then, that an intermezzo became a favorite dramatic form, since it allowed the guests some time to recover between courses. The intermezzi were sometimes fanciful

NAVE DI AMERIGO VESPVCCI INTERMEDIO QVARTO

pastorals with songs and dances, sometimes five-act comedies or tragedies with musical interludes. Following a fashion introduced at the Spanish court, the courtiers themselves often took minor roles in these elaborate productions.

Since they were obliged to spend much of the year at court, members of the English nobility generally maintained townhouses in London. To ward off boredom, they contrived entertainments, vying with one another in the sumptuous presentation of the latest plays, music, and dances from Italy. Nothing so suited the courtiers' love of intrigue and admiration for personal cleverness as did the masque, an extravagant spectacle built upon the pastoral. The creators of these revels, perfectly aware that the pastoral was the European offspring of the ancient satyr play, used it to make light of court scandals or secrets. They frequently chose a classical allegory or myth that bore some similarity to the scandal or secret in question, drawing out the parallel in a flamboyant conceit that required lavish costumes and settings. The masque presented two tantalizing enigmas: it hid the scandal from the ignorant, and, since the aristocrats who took part wore masks, it hid their true identities. One can appreciate the attraction this dangerous form of theater held for the Renaissance courtier, who, stimulated by the prevailing atmosphere of self-confident individualism, used every artifice to gain and maintain personal power. The masque, so often dismissed as unimportant and puzzling in present-day productions of Renaissance plays, is in fact the most perfect expression of the cabalistic spirit of intrigue that permeated Renaissance life.

In time, of course, the lavishness of the masque was to prove financially disastrous for the courts of Europe, most of which were still supported by an outmoded and inadequate system of feudal taxes. Real wealth lay in the hands of the rising merchant class, and consequently it was they who were to become the true patrons of sixteenth-century theater. English merchants flourished under royal charter, and they were soon recognized everywhere as a distinguished breed of traders—the aristocrats of the commercial world. Far more interested in lasting

An intermezzo "happening" during banquets eased the digestion and slowed down the intake of courtly diners—both in Italy, where the custom began, and later in England. Above left, a drawing of an intermezzo during the 1608 wedding festivities of the prince of Tuscany shows the bringing forth of Amerigo Vespucci's ship. The masque, a much more elaborate theater piece, afforded courtly Englishmen a chance to dress up and dance in disguise. In 1605 Inigo Jones was put in charge of court masques, and some of his costume designs appear opposite.

gains than in turning a quick profit, they established themselves as experts, advising their countrymen in the selection of Italian art and then arranging for its purchase and importation. They themselves eventually became patrons of the arts—evaluating art in both aesthetic and monetary terms.

As representatives of the power of wealth, the merchant class exercised a strong and distinctive influence upon taste. While Venetian and Florentine merchant princes entertained hopes of being accepted into the titled aristocracy, the English merchant was proud of his middle-class status. He knew that power lay in money rather than in titles, and he supported whatever recommended his way of life to his fellow men. His community mindedness in education, politics, and religion sprang not from a Platonic humanism but from a tradesman's belief in the ultimate profits of long-term investments. He was not a philosopher but a realist who loved seeing everyday life portrayed on the stage. Part of William Shakespeare's genius was that he, more than any of his fellow playwrights, was sensitive to that fact, and as a result his plays contain plain-spoken, mundane characters as well as philosophical, heroic ones. This capacity for characterization was a skill that Shakespeare shared with the prepotent genius of Spain's golden age of theater, Lope de Vega. Both were aware of the different tastes of noblemen and merchants; both disliked the disruptive groundlings who made up the bulk

of their audiences in the public theater; and both provided scenes to please all members of their audiences.

The new spirit of personal initiative and private enterprise very quickly asserted itself in the theater. For many centuries all theater in Europe, except that performed by bands of traveling players, had been a community affair, largely under the aegis of the Church. In England, Spain, and France, municipalities had licensed charitable fraternities to produce their local plays, long after the Church had ceased to sanction theater performances. These brotherhoods were tax free, and their considerable income was used to support hospitals, foundling homes, and alms houses. And when religious plays fell from favor, enterprising minds realized the commercial potential of secular theater. The first commercial theater company in France was licensed in Lyon and installed in a new Italian-style theater building in 1540. Thirty-six years later, James Burbage, a London carpenter with an eye for business, built a playhouse called The Theater in Finsbury Fields, about a mile beyond the city limits. In Madrid the great Italian actor-manager Ganassa took a ten-year lease on an innyard, converted it into a playhouse, and in 1583 inaugurated the Teatro del Corral de la Pacheca. Needless to say, once these first secular theaters were established, others sprang up to compete for the burgeoning playgoing public.

There is an abundance of information about admission prices and receipts in commercial theaters of this period, but it is difficult to assign modern values to the figures. At that time, money in general was worth about thirty times more than it is now, and there are many other considerations that complicate any sort of comparison of ancient and modern currencies. One factor was to remain constant throughout the centuries, however, and it was that when a production was a hit it made a great deal of money for its producers, while unpopular plays

Elizabethan London welcomed drama. In the sixteenth-century engraving above, itinerant actors perform on street stages while other players enter a nearby inn for refreshment. In Visscher's superb 1616 panorama of the English capital (below), both the Swan and Globe theaters are visible along the lower margin.

were financial disasters. From the beginning, attendance was the barometer, and in the sixteenth century in particular there was a constant demand for new plays. As a result, even when a play was successful its running time was relatively short by modern standards.

At the end of the sixteenth century no capital city in Western Europe demonstrated the tonic effects of the new humanism on urban life more dramatically than did London. Cut off from the Continent by the English Channel, the British had been obliged to become expert seafarers and traders, and by the Elizabethan age trade had become their lifeblood. In competition with the Venetians and Florentines, they had established an international network of trading houses with agents and warehouses in virtually every commercial port, and London's docks were a treasury of exotic goods. England seemed destined to shed her medieval status—that of a third-rate political and commercial power—and with the spectacular defeat of the Spanish Armada in 1588, she did indeed become the greatest mercantile power in the world.

The language of London's streets, reflecting as it did the growing conflict between acquisitive liberalism and cautious conservatism, provided a perfect dramatic idiom, rich and colorful in vocabulary, terse and aphoristic in syntax. Burbage's theater had been in operation for a decade, and a new playhouse, the Rose, which Philip Henslowe was about to inaugurate on the banks of the Thames, would soon provide it with strong competition. The plays themselves were provided by a new group of playwrights, just arrived from Cambridge and Oxford and known as the University Wits–Robert Greene, Thomas Nashe, George Peele, Christopher Marlowe, and John Lyly. And, most importantly, their company was augmented by two young poets who had never been to the university: the talented Thomas Kyd and a young Warwickshireman named William Shakespeare. Everything was in readiness for the

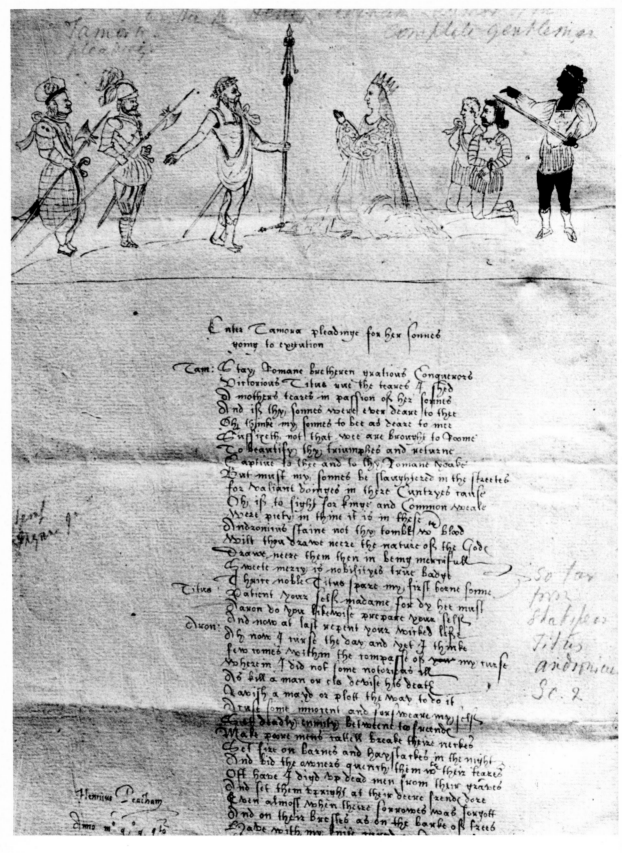

Tamora
pleadinge

compleate gentleman

Enter Tamora pleadinge for her sonnes
goinge to execution

Tam: Stay Romane bretheren gratious Conquerors
Victorious Titus rue the teares 4 shed
O mothers teares in passion of her sonnes
And iff thy sonnes wewel euer deare to thee
Oh, thinke my sonnes to bee as deare to mee
Sufficeth not that wee are brought to Roome
To beautifye thy triumphes and returne
Captiue to thee and to thy Romane Noake
But must my sonnes be slaughtered in the streetes
for Valiant doinges in there Cuntryes cause
Oh iff to fight for kinge and Common weale
Were piety in thine it is in these
Andronicus staine not thy tombe with blood
Wilt thou drawe neere the nature off the Gods
Drawe neere them then in being mercifull
Sweete mercy is nobilityes true badge
Thrise noble Titus spare my first borne sonne

Titus   Patient your self madame for dy hee must
Aaron do you likewise prepare your self
Aaron: And now at last repent your wicked liffe

Oh now 4 curse the day and yet 4 thinke
few romes within the compasse off my curse
Wherein 4 did not some notorious ill
As kill a man or els deuise his death
Rauish a mayde or plott the way to do it
Accuse some innocent and forsweare my selfe
Sett deadly enmity betweene to freende
Make poore mens cattell breake theire neckes
Sett fire on barnes and haystackes in the night
And bid the owners quench them with theire teares
Oft haue 4 digd vp dead men from their graues
And set them vprights at their deere freends doore
Euen almost when theire sorrowes was forgott
And on theire breasts as on the barke off treese
Haue with my knife

Henricus Peacham
Anno mº qº qº 1º

So far
wm
Shakspeare
Titus
andronicus
Sc. 2

great age of theater that was to follow.

No one had yet shown how the vigorous action of the late medieval plays, with their hearty humor and dour wisdom, could be effectively crossed with the formal structure of the classics to produce a healthy new species of drama. The long-awaited answer was provided in the opening days of the winter season of 1586 with the presentation at the Rose of Marlowe's *Tamburlaine the Great, Part I*. It has been called "the most momentous performance in the history of English theater," for in *Tamburlaine* the twenty-three-year-old Marlowe had succeeded in producing that robust, genial hybrid: the Elizabethan play.

In *Tamburlaine the Great* Marlowe employed neither the rough-and-tumble comedy style of the English Cycle plays nor the stiff, unnatural formalism of the schoolmen's tragedies. Instead, he hit upon a solution that was to serve as a model for a generation of playwrights: the admixture of titanic, episodic action with classic form, the whole expressed in powerful blank verse.

Shakespeare, only twenty-three himself and already an accomplished poet, certainly saw one of the early performances of *Tamburlaine*; indeed, some think it was this that led him to become a playwright. He had actually come down to London to join the Queen's Company as an actor, but his talents as a writer were quickly appreciated and put to use. By 1593 he had written five plays, the most noteworthy of which were *Titus Andronicus*, his answer to the challenge of *Tamburlaine*, and *Richard III*.

Between 1593 and 1612 Shakespeare was to write at least one play a year, and sometimes as many as three. Such a sustained outpouring of dramatic writing was prodigious enough, but no one in the history of world theater had ever demonstrated such mastery of dramatic poetry, such breadth and versatility of imagination, as Shakespeare did in the thirty-seven plays he wrote in scarcely twenty-five years. In the "wooden O" of the Elizabethan playhouse he created a universe of human destinies where contesting kingdoms war and feuding households clash with heroic energy, where ambitious men rise and fall in a bloody agony of love, revenge, and perversity, dragging down with them the guilty and the innocent alike. It is a world in which the action leaps with surprising sureness from scene to scene, releasing in its entirety the rich imagery of Elizabethan speech.

Shakespeare had begun his playwrighting career by rewriting an old play, *Henry VI*, which he fashioned into three parts with incredible speed between 1591 and 1592. The next year he wrote *Richard III* and *Titus Andronicus*, and shortly thereafter he began his apprenticeship in comedy with *The Comedy of Errors*, patterned after Plautus' *Menaechmi*. *The Taming of the Shrew* followed, then came *Two Gentlemen of Verona*, and next, *Love's Labour's Lost*, which is believed to be his first original plot.

One of the most remarkable aspects of Shakespeare's genius was his versatility. During 1595 he wrote the great lyric tragedy *Romeo and Juliet*, the poignant history of *Richard II*, and his incomparable fantasy, *A Midsummer Night's Dream*. Given another old play to rework, he produced *King John*; then, drawing upon Italian sources and using

As a young married man and father, William Shakespeare journeyed from bucolic Stratford to cosmopolitan London to begin an acting career. Several years later he wrote Titus Andronicus. *The manuscript page opposite, copied from the original, was illustrated and signed by Henry Peacham in the year 1595.*

Overleaf: *Macbeth has met his witches in countless ways; here they huddle before him in a fanciful nineteenth-century painting.*

details concerning the contemporary execution in Portugal of the Jew Roderigo Lopez, he wrote *The Merchant of Venice*. Shakespeare also seems to have been an excellent businessman, one who could make new plays from old and turn topical interests to profit. Aware of the great public interest in national history, for example, he repeatedly made use of the 1587 edition of Raphael Holinshed's *Chronicles of England*, the source, for example, of *Henry IV, Parts I and II*. It is in these plays that Shakespeare introduced Sir John Falstaff, the most famous comic figure in English literature, and with him a world of low-life comic characters who immediately won the hearts of London theater-goers. A few months later he created the disdainful Beatrice and the impressionable Benedick of *Much Ado About Nothing*, two of his most popular characters with Elizabethan audiences. In answer to public demand for an "English" play—and once again using Holinshed's *Chronicles* as a source—he wrote the brilliantly nationalistic *Henry V*, which, with its masterful chorus, its noble king, its swarm of outspoken commoners, its balance of seriousness and levity, sincerity and irony, pomp and plainness, tells us more about the Elizabethan era and its theater than any other single play.

In 1598, supposedly in answer to the queen's request for a play showing Falstaff in love, Shakespeare wrote *The Merry Wives of Windsor*. The play is not one of his best, yet it is a most perceptive depiction of the rising middle class—its aspirations, its healthy sense of humor, its increasing sense of security and responsibility. Shakespeare's treatment of Falstaff is a perfect example of how Elizabethan playwrights borrowed stock characters from the classics, in this case crossing Plautus' miles gloriosus, the braggart soldier, with the old man Senex, and invested them with a new identity and vitality.

After the decidedly "English" *Henry V* and *Merry Wives*, Shakespeare wrote what many critics consider his most "classic" tragedy, *Julius Caesar*. The play is almost devoid of that comic relief that mitigates and often enhances most of his tragic works, and, in this respect, it is most atypical. (Significantly, the neoclassicists of the seventeenth and eighteenth centuries, who tampered with so many of Shakespeare's plays, tailoring them to suit their formalistic tastes, left *Caesar* untouched.)

With the writing, in 1600, of the romantic, song-filled comedies *As You Like It* and *Twelfth Night*, Shakespeare ended the great period of his lyrical comedies and histories. He was to write more comedies, but never again would the tone be as light and poetic. He was thirty-six and, in the considered opinion of his contemporaries, the greatest writer of his day. Through wise investment, he had become a man of property in both London and his native Stratford, and he owned stock in the Lord Chamberlain's Men, the acting company for which he wrote and acted.

Many explanations have been offered for the distinct change in tone found in Shakespeare's plays after 1600. This emphatic shift may simply have reflected the playwright's growing interest in tragedy, but it is also likely that Shakespeare, like so many other Elizabethans who

The jolly soldier Falstaff inspects recruits in the scene opposite from Henry IV *as painted by William Hogarth. Although Prince Hal did not attend Falstaff's deathbed in Shakespeare's version of the legend, he did exactly that in the vision (right) of artist Francis Wheatley.*

had put much store in the popular Earl of Essex, was deeply and permanently affected by the young earl's dramatic fall from royal favor and his tragic end. The change of tone is already apparent in some of Feste's songs in *Twelfth Night*, and in *Hamlet*, written in 1601, we perceive a more sober and serious view of life. The bitter *Troilus and Cressida*, the ironic *All's Well That Ends Well*, and the puzzling *Measure for Measure*—as well as *Timon of Athens*, *Pericles*, *Cymbeline*, *A Winter's Tale*, and *The Tempest*, all written between 1601 and 1612—demonstrate the playwright's darkening attitude toward life. This was, after all, the period in which Shakespeare wrote his greatest tragedies. *Hamlet* was followed by *Othello* in 1602, *King Lear* and *Macbeth* in 1605, and *Antony and Cleopatra* and *Coriolanus* in the next two years. Although he collaborated with John Fletcher in writing *Henry VIII* and *The Two Noble Kinsmen*, *The Tempest*, written in 1611, was Shakespeare's eloquent valedictory. He died in 1616 at the age of fifty-two.

Almost half a century before the brilliant Elizabethan epoch, the Spanish were already enjoying their own golden age. They too created an era of unprecedented literary greatness, a time when the theater in Iberia reached its apogee. The great Sevillian actor-playwright Lope de la Rueda, progenitor of the *Siglo de Oro*, had traveled widely in Spain during the sixteenth century. Playing on a stage improvised from market trestles, he established the ground rules for the rude prose comedies that the genius Lope de Vega was later to fashion into an elegant genre. It was also Lope de la Rueda who invented the *género chico*, the Spanish interlude, which writers such as Cervantes would later perfect.

68

Consider the range of Shakespeare's dramatic imagination—from Ophelia, sinking innocently to her death (left), to the guilt-ridden Lady Macbeth crowning herself queen (played by Ellen Terry, right). The painting of Ophelia is by John Everett Millais; that of Lady Macbeth by John Singer Sargent. From the seventeenth century on, women were permitted to play female roles on London stages. At left, below is a scene from A Midsummer Night's Dream as engraved by M. Smith.

Just as Marlowe is credited with inventing the Elizabethan play, Lope de Vega can be called the inventor of the Spanish national drama. Lope de Vega was born in Madrid in 1562, the son of an artisan who loved letters, and as a result the young Lope was writing verses at five and plays at ten. Sent to a Jesuit school, he received a good classical education and subsequently took holy orders. A passionate man in life and letters, Lope was probably "the greatest literary improviser the world has ever seen." He could write a play in two days, and, in his most active period, he regularly produced two plays a week. He wrote more than eighteen hundred plays, of which five hundred have survived. His energies were gargantuan: he is known to have had many love affairs, to have kept up two households, to have served as personal secretary for four noblemen simultaneously, to have maintained an enormous correspondence with his numerous friends, to have traveled widely and often, to have been a faithful visitor to hospitals, and to have attended religious services every day. Small wonder that Cervantes referred to him as "a monster of nature."

Unlike his contemporary, Shakespeare, Lope de Vega was a realist who rarely delved beneath the surface of situations, yet his plays possess a sense of community not seen in theater since the time of the ancient Greeks. This sense is clearly present in his greatest play, *Fuenteovejuna*, in which a small village rebels against an unjust military governor, kills him, and is pardoned by the king.

Forced to write at such an inhuman pace, Lope scorned most of his plays as moneymakers and longed to devote himself to more considered literary pursuits, but the material necessities of two households and numerous natural children kept him busy. Because he chose to write in the popular idiom, Lope was summarily dismissed by the literary cliques of Spain, but the theatergoing public adored him. Everywhere he went ordinary people showed him the sort of adulation that the Spanish still shower upon popular singing stars and bullfighters. He was an extraordinary contradiction: a priest with two households and many children, a man with an enormous appetite for life and yet a penitent with a deep love of religion. Perhaps it was just such contradictions that so endeared him to ordinary people.

The other great theatrical genius of the Spanish golden age was Pedro Calderón de la Barca, who was born in 1600 and who dominated

the Spanish court stages for almost forty years. A formal and baroque writer and an incomparable master of artistic language, Calderón de la Barca wrote plays that were completely different in spirit from Lope de Vega's—intellectual, deeply religious, and philosophical. Like Lope, he received a classical education from the Jesuits, yet instead of taking holy orders at once he chose the stage and the life of an adventurous, brawling gallant. In time, Calderón became one of Philip IV's favorites and was chosen to write the principal piece, *El mayor encanto, Amor* (*Love, the Greatest Delight*), for the inauguration of Philip's new palace, the Buen Retiro. A sudden change of heart when he was forty caused him to take holy orders and retire from public life. By that time Calderón had written some one hundred and twenty plays, eighty religious allegories, and twenty minor pieces. Among them are two of the greatest masterpieces of world theater literature: *La vida es sueño* (*Life Is a Dream*) and *El alcalde de Zalamea* (*The Mayor of Zalamea*).

The actor-playwrights of the sixteenth and seventeenth centuries, whether English or Spanish, had very little legal protection against plagiarism. Their works were usually registered, but it was almost impossible to prevent envious competitors from filching plays and rewriting them as their own. Managers kept a close watch on audiences to see that no one was busily taking notes in shorthand, a frequent means of lifting speeches and scenes. And acting companies, determined to protect their

Spain's two greatest playwrights each produced more plays than England's Shakespeare. Below are frontispieces from the comedies of Lope de Vega (left) and Calderón de la Barca (right). A scene from El rayo, la piedra, el fuego *(left), one of some two hundred works by Calderón, was engraved from a 1652 sketch.*

integrity, began to incorporate, selling shares and claiming some noble or powerful person as their patron. Playwrights commonly sold their works outright to a company, and sometimes, as in the case of Shakespeare, the playwright actually bought shares in the company that produced his plays. Copyright laws were slow to evolve, and for many years acting companies saw no profit in having their plays printed. Prompt books were made for performances, but once the productions were retired, the plays were either rewritten or lost. Fortunately, two factors have preserved Shakespeare's plays: their immense popularity, which kept them in the repertory, and the fact that during Shakespeare's lifetime, stationers began to buy the printing rights to his plays, insuring their permanence in print.

The established actor in Shakespeare's day probably enjoyed more social acceptance than he had since ancient Greek times. But such was not the case with all performers. In order to escape a thousand-year-old legal prejudice against them, actors had to establish themselves in licensed companies under the protection of powerful patrons; only then could they be considered legitimate. The unprecedented appearance in 1576 of Burbage's theater, a freestanding private playhouse in the suburbs of London, and its immediate success with the public, called for a special set of laws. Before the opening of the theater, plays had been performed in the inner courts of inns and in private halls. Queen Elizabeth I was quick to prescribe a set of regulations: no play was to treat religion or politics, nor could a play be publicly or privately performed without the license of the mayor or chief officers. Further, no public performance was to begin later than two o'clock in the afternoon, so that the audience might get safely home before dark. The city itself imposed numerous regulations to protect the public against immorality, quarrels, fights and general riots, and theft and fraud at such performances. New statutes defined responsibility in cases of injury caused by the collapse of stages, scenic effects, or galleries, and against fires caused by weapons and gunpowder used in plays.

In our own day rhetoric is so out of fashion that the very word carries a pejorative connotation, but in sixteenth- and seventeenth-century Europe, rhetoric—the ancient Greek art of persuasive speaking—enjoyed tremendous prestige, so much so that the mastering of rhetoric was considered vital to educated discourse. It was taught to every grammar school student, and every major playwright of the era—whether English, French, Spanish, or Italian—clearly demonstrates his debt to rhetoric in his knowledge of its rules. The best actors of the period were also perfectly aware of these rules and were ready at the drop of a hat to demonstrate their skills in the extempore composition of speeches. Following the rhetorical laws of delivery, they developed a complete chironomy—that is, a pattern of hand movements by which they dramatized both individual words and the general emotional tone of their speeches.

During Shakespeare's time, acting was to evolve from the static, elocutionary delivery inherited from the rhetoricians to a "lively style," one characterized by a more lifelike interpretation of the lines of both verse and prose passages. There can be no doubt that Shakespeare, himself an actor, was interested in instituting a very specific style of delivery. It

75

takes no stretch of the imagination to understand Hamlet's advice to the players as Shakespeare's own, for at the end of his very explicit criticism of the usual "robustious, periwig-pated fellow tear[ing] a passion to tatters, to very rags, to split the ears of the groundlings" he adds the admonition, "O! reform it all."

In essence, Hamlet's speech was a plea for subtlety, one provoked by the fact that the Elizabethan actor was compelled to deliver his lines from the apron of the open stage in broad daylight. With no stage lighting and almost no scenic effects, he had to set the stage and create the place, time, situation, character, and action through his own skill. Moreover, he stood within easy range of nutshells, orange skins, and apple cores, should his performance give offense to the gaping groundlings. Such vulnerability demanded that the actor be skilled in playing to every level of society represented at the performance. It should be added that those groundlings, who paid half a day's wages to stand for two hours at a play, were predisposed to be pleased. No contemporary event in London or Madrid, whether bullbaiting, bearbaiting, or cockfights, is reckoned to have drawn such crowds as did plays. Shakespeare occasionally openly scorns the groundlings as dolts, and Lope de Vega complains bitterly in his correspondence about the bawling, disruptive "seated Spaniard"; but both authors consistently succeeded in attracting record crowds to the theater with their ability to write in a popular style that drew applause from the uneducated standees on the one hand and produced finespun lyricism on the other. Consequently, it can be argued, both playwrights must have found actors who were able to satisfy the requirements of such versatility in style.

Until well into the seventeenth century, women were forbidden to appear on the English stage, although they were a common sight in

The setting in the eighteenth-century reproduction of an Elizabethan theatrical scene at right, below, has a shape reminiscent of the Greek skene. English theatrical audiences ranged from such notables as Queen Elizabeth I herself (above) to the dandy shown in the portrait opposite, to the raucous poor.

tectum

porticus

sedilia

orchestra

ingressus

mimorum
ædes.

proscænium

planities siue arena.

Ex obseruationibus Londinensibus
Iohannis de witt

The Swan theater, sketched by Jan de Witt in 1596 (opposite), forty-two years after its opening, incorporated the circle of the Greek threshing floor. Built upon it was a proscenium stage with front, middle, and rear portions—the last of which was roofed by the upper stage. Galleries also extended around three sides. The Globe theater—seen above in a twentieth-century conjectural drawing—was built in 1599 and charged various prices: a penny to stand in the pit, two to stand in the galleries, and three for a seat.

France, and, to a certain extent, in Spain. In England, all women's parts were played by young boys. In fact, troupes of young actors, known as children's companies, most of them attached to cathedral schools and under powerful patronage, were so popular with the public that they constituted a real financial threat to the other acting companies.

In London the first conventional playhouse was created, as we have seen, by an enterprising carpenter, who built his theater beyond the city limits to escape the Lord Mayor's opposition. Precious little is known about the structure of the theater. We do know that bearbaiting and bullbaiting and other kinds of entertainments were given there and that the timbers from the building were later used to build the more famous Globe. Likewise, we know very little about the structural peculiarities of the Rose, the Curtain, the Hope, or the Fortune—all theaters built during this period, and all subsequently destroyed. As luck would have it, however, a Dutchman named Jan de Witt visited London in 1596 and made a drawing of the Swan, the largest of these playhouses, for his *Book of Commonplaces*. A copy of this drawing, made by a fellow student, still exists—the only extant contemporary drawing of the interior of an Elizabethan playhouse. The sketch is crude, but it shows quite clearly the circular arrangement of the three galleries and the pit, or ground, around the thrust stage where the groundlings stood. The only property on the stage is a rude bench. There are no scene effects. Upstage, a roofed area with two doors and an upper gallery support a tiny roof from which the flag waves, indicating that a play is in progress. We are inclined to think of these theaters as small, yet the Swan, which was perhaps larger than most, could accommodate three thousand spectators.

There were, of course, private playhouses set up in great halls, and there was the Blackfriars, a theater arrangement within the refectory of a former monastery, as well as the rude accommodations in the Inns of Court, frequented by students. It is noteworthy, however, that the English playhouse, a real commercial venture, freestanding and stable, is unique in that it sprang from moneymaking exigencies. It made no effort to copy an ancient model, nor was it lavish in the Palladian manner. It was an independent enterprise, but one that perfectly reflected the astonishing vigor and unorthodox inventions of England's greatest age of theater.

5

Renaissance in France, Restoration in England

THE GENERAL ATMOSPHERE OF LIFE in England changed with the death of Queen Elizabeth I in 1603, as if the queen herself had been the embodiment of the considered elegance and good sense of the era that took her name. Any successor would have suffered by comparison, but James I—ugly and suspicious, and a pedantic, arrogant defender of the divine right of kings—was an especially poor substitute for the shrewd, popular, eloquent old queen. James was, however, an even greater lover of the theater than Elizabeth had been. Imitating French and Italian court fashion, he produced numerous masques and spent fabulous sums on their presentation. In 1604, the first year of his reign, he attached all the London acting companies and their theaters to the Revel's Office at court—and there is no denying that such official patronage was financially beneficial for both playwrights and actors.

Shakespeare and Ben Jonson were to remain among the new king's favorite playwrights despite the fact that their dramas continued to reflect the style of the Elizabethan age. Newer playwrights such as John Marston, Thomas Middleton, and John Webster, on the other hand, set their plays in the affluent, cynical Jacobean world, and the baroque, passionate richness of their intricate and perverse creations has never been equaled.

Although the king's patronage was of great advantage to the theater and eventually paved the way for the establishment of several royal academies, it proved to be politically disastrous. The Stuart monarchs —James and his unfortunate successor, Charles I—not only lacked Elizabeth's wisdom and political astuteness, they also made a point of irritating their opponents through the medium of plays and theatricals. The playwrights of the period were notorious Puritan baiters, and as the Puritans gained political strength they began to retaliate. When the predictable split between the established church and the dissenters took place, the theater was therefore in double jeopardy—for theater was not only held by the Puritans to be an occasion of sin and the devil's tool, but was also attached by royal decree to the monarch, the church's nominal head and the Puritans' archfoe.

Charles I came to the throne in 1624. Continuing his father's policy of arrogant harassment of the Puritans, he allowed his wife, Henrietta Maria, to present a group of French actresses at the Blackfriars in 1629. These women were "booed, hissed, and apple-pelted off" the stage, but

the scandal gave rise to wide criticism—especially since the queen had intended to appear with the actresses in the play. William Prynne, a Puritan author, wrote a scathing denunciation of players in a mock pastoral which he entitled *Histriomastix*. His shot must have hit the mark, for he was punished by the king's secret court, which pilloried him and cut off his ears.

On September 2, 1642, the Puritan-dominated Parliament officially suppressed stage plays. While this Act of Suppression was not absolutely effective, it was implemented and re-enacted in both 1647 and 1648, depriving actors of their legitimate living. Following the execution of Charles I in 1649, the royal household fled into exile in France. For the next eighteen years there was of course no official subvention of the English theater, and most of the old theaters, including Shakespeare's Globe, were pulled down.

The court of Louis XIII, which received the English royal household during its years in exile, was not as flamboyant as the French court had once been. The king was himself a sober and abstemious person who disliked the Italianate ostentation that had been introduced by the Medici queens, and while he permitted his mother, Marie de Médicis, to indulge her Italian love for extravagant spectacles, he refused to take part in them. It was Cardinal Richelieu, the king's all-powerful minister and adviser, who gave official support to these spectacles while simultaneously creating the master plan for his country's future greatness. Not only was the cardinal indulgent toward "things humanist and Italian," he also saw in the fabulous court celebrations and ballets he staged a means of building national prestige. He consequently took a very active part in the planning and execution of these spectacles, prescribing in detail what was desired. In fact, it is Richelieu who is credited with having first divided the performing area from the audience, confining the action of the spectacles to the stage.

As the foremost patrons of the French theater, Louis XIII and Cardinal Richelieu were privileged to sit in the orchestra itself at performances in the Petit Bourbon Palace (left, below). Parisians of the next generation (above) frequently sat much closer to the stage. Outdoors, aristocratic spectacles continued. Opposite, a théâtre de l'eau arrangement in a corner of the woods at Versailles, as imaginatively recreated by Jean Cotelle.

In spite of his father's dislike of court spectacle, the young Louis XIV, encouraged by his own adviser, Cardinal Mazarin, took great pleasure in extravaganzas and ceremony. Thus Richelieu and Mazarin were jointly responsible for initiating and supporting a policy of royal patronage of theater in France by sponsoring entertainments that identified France with the person of the king; indeed, Louis XIV first laid claim to the title of Sun King in a court ballet when he was fifteen. This royal patronage eventually led to the establishment of national theaters under state subsidy.

The presentation of lavish court spectacles was not the only form of theatrical activity that flourished in seventeenth-century France, however. In the middle years of the century, Pierre Corneille and Jean Racine created a new and decidedly French form of tragedy, one that demanded, as Granville Barker says, "the fierce intellectual integrity to which the French mind may be aroused." The English had by this time already tried their hand at writing tragedies. Their great tragic works are distinctly English, working as they do through contrast, variety, and multiplicity—brushing aside the classic Aristotelian unities of time, place, action, and character, and preferring deeply human identities to heroic ones.

The beginnings of French tragedy were stormy, if only because the ideas of the playwrights themselves ran head on into the theories of no less influential a personage than Richelieu. Richelieu's interest in academies as arbiters of national taste suggests that he wished, like some of the Medici before him, to determine and foster certain cultural ideals, among them a French theater based on classic models. He favored the *Poetics* of Aristotle, which was the foundation of the tragic unities, and

like most theoreticians, he believed that great tragedies could be written by applying certain aesthetic rules to the task. Ironically, in trying to impose guidelines on the French theater, Richelieu ignored, or perhaps simply distrusted, the French genius—that set of characteristics that immediately identify an artistic creation as French.

Richelieu's misunderstanding of the true genesis of national theater can be seen in his quarrels with the great Pierre Corneille over the importance of the Aristotelian unities. With the help of his famous Committee of Five—five well-known playwrights, of whom Corneille was one—Richelieu had written several tragedies, all of them elaborate affairs strongly influenced by Italian court entertainments, and all of them unsuccessful. Corneille so disagreed with Richelieu over this way of writing tragedy that after the production of his own *Médée* the frustrated playwright left Paris and retired to his native Rouen. He did return to Paris two years later, however, to present *Le Cid* at the Théâtre du Marais. Corneille's friend Montdory, who was that theater's managing director and leading actor, took the role of Rodrigue, the play's young hero.

Although *Le Cid* broke with the classic aesthetics of tragedy, it achieved poetic heights that were unparalleled in the history of French drama. The play's immediate success infuriated Richelieu and his academicians, who roundly condemned the work. As a result Corneille was obliged to wait ten years to be admitted to the Académie Française. In the interim he continued to write other remarkable works: *Horace* in 1640, *Cinna* in 1641, *Polyeucte* a year or so later. His *Andromède* was produced at the Petit Bourbon Théâtre in Paris in 1650—against the

Pierre Corneille's 1636 tragicomedy Le Cid *was still popular two hundred years later when Elisa Felix (left, below), better known as Rachel, took the role of Chimène. Jean Baptiste Racine's only comedy,* Les Plaideurs, *concerned the character Dandin, a role played by Baptiste Cade (above). Racine's last play,* Athalie, *featured Marie Françoise Dumesnil and a Mr. Brizard, both seen in the watercolor at right. Voltaire's protégé, Henri Louis Lekain (left, above) acts a part in the play* Manlius *with an unknown companion.*

Actors
Elisa felix (Rachael)
Baptiste Cade
Marie Francoise Dumesnil
Henri Louis Lekain

Molière | Jodelet | Poisson | Turlupin | Le Capitain Matamore | Arlequin | Guillot Gorju | Gros Guillaume | Gaultier Garguille | Le Dottor Grazian Balourd | polichinelle | Pantalon | Scaramouche | Philippin | Briquelle | Trivelin

sumptuous backdrops that Giacomo Torelli had created three years earlier for a spectacular production of *Orpheus*. Torelli's fabulous machinery and setting, which was totally out of accord with Corneille's splendidly restrained and quietly classical work, lent an incongruous aura to the entire production.

Jean Racine, thirty-three years younger than le grand Corneille, declared himself the older playwright's rival in 1664, the year he sprang to prominence with *La Thébaïde*. Yet Racine, for all his arrogance toward Corneille, built his tragedies upon the model that Corneille had provided, producing in succession seven of the masterpieces of Western theatrical history: *Andromaque* in 1667; *Les Plaideurs*, based on Aristophanes' *Wasps*, in 1668; *Britannicus* a year later; and then *Bérénice*, *Bajazet*, and *Mithridate* within a year of each other. *Iphigénie* followed in 1674, and finally, in 1677, the splendid masterpiece *Phèdre*. Because of his great chagrin over the critical failure of *Phèdre*, Racine retired from playwriting to become historian and biographer to Louis XIV, and he did not write another play until 1689. Then, at the request of the king's longtime mistress and second wife, Madame de Maintenon, he wrote *Esther* for the young ladies at her school at St. Cyr. Madame de Maintenon was so pleased with the results that she prevailed upon Racine to write another play for the school. The result was *Athalie*, produced in 1691.

Corneille and Racine are, indisputably, giants in the history of French theater, but Molière is without doubt the greatest comic playwright Western Europe ever produced. The Paris-born Molière's early

education in the theater was acquired from the troupes of Italian actors who had come to France with the Medici queens. If the French had learned much from those Italian troupes, the Italian players, in turn, had learned from the French. Their playing had become more refined, inculcating the literary aspects of plot construction, fixed dialogue, and predetermined action. And because their amended style was a perfect vehicle for criticizing the self-importance of the French, the more talented Italian players were soon able to install themselves in theaters of their own in Paris and other major cities. The most famous of these companies, the Comédie Italienne, took up residence in the historic Hôtel de Bourgogne and enjoyed enormous popularity and financial success until it incurred the wrath of the prudish Madame de Maintenon. A thinly veiled caricature of her in *La Fausse Prude* so infuriated la Maintenon that she had the offending play closed by royal proclamation in 1697. The Comédie Italienne was henceforth forbidden to play within twenty leagues of Paris, a ban that lasted for many years and actually broke the troupe's hold on the Paris public.

In 1643, the year that Louis XIV, then age five, ascended the French throne, Jean-Baptiste Poquelin, a twenty-one-year-old law student at the Jesuit College of Clermont, abandoned his studies, joined a theatrical troupe called the Illustre-Théâtre, and changed his name to Molière. The Illustre-Théâtre met with scant success, and Molière was forced to tour the provinces for thirteen miserable years, playing improvised farces in commedia dell'arte style. The young Molière lost little time in becoming the leader of this luckless company, and he wrote most of its material. In 1658 the company returned to Paris, where

Seventeenth-century actors who appeared separately at the Théâtre Royal in Paris are depicted together in the stage line-up at left, above. They include the great actor-author Molière at the far left. In the engraving above, Molière's character le bourgeois gentilhomme is played by Jourdain. The engraving at lower left is a scene from Molière's Tartuffe; the painting at right is a version of the death of Scapino, Molière's quick-witted, unprincipled servant.

it played Corneille's *Nicomède* to a very tepid reception. Its performance of *The Doctor in Love*, one of Molière's own works, caught the favor of the young king, however, and with such powerful patronage Molière's company was soon installed in the Petit Bourbon. For a number of years Molière's players shared their theater with the Italian company of Tiberio Fiorillo, creator of the famous Scaramouche, but in 1660 the company was able to move to the theater of the Palais-Royal itself.

Although Molière enjoyed royal favor throughout his life and wrote one brilliant comedy after another—any one of which might have assured him a place in theater history—he was never able to achieve personal happiness. At forty he married his leading lady, Armande Béjart, the youngest sister of Madeleine Béjart, the woman for whom he had abandoned his law studies in the first place and with whose family he had toured the provinces during the period between 1643 and 1658. The marriage was not a happy one, with two sons dying in infancy. Only a daughter, Esprit, survived and she became a mainstay of Molière's last years. Since he was unwilling to give up acting, of which he was passionately fond, the prolific playwright was never elected to the Académie Française. The brilliant roster of his plays recommends him for more universal honor, however; it is hard to think of any international repertory without *Tartuffe, The Misanthrope, The Miser, The Learned Ladies, The Imaginary Invalid, The Doctor in*

Spite of Himself, or *Le Bourgeois Gentilhomme.* Molière himself was playing Argan in *The Imaginary Invalid* on February 17, 1673, when he collapsed on stage and died.

Under these three great figures, Corneille, Racine, and Molière, the French theater came of age in the short period between 1636 and 1699. It produced the tragédie classique, a distinctly French form built on classic references, and it created the French comedy, just as French in nature as the tragedies but built on commedia dell'arte techniques and interspersed at times with another genre, the ballet interlude, which derived from Italian court influences.

After the death of Cromwell, the English court returned to London in 1660, bringing with it many tastes acquired in France. Charles II entered London with the greatest show of pomp and ceremony that the English had ever seen, a display that seemed all the more impressive after the sober Puritan interlude. Thus the Restoration began with great fanfare and the determined imposition of tastes more French than English. Like his predecessor, the ill-fated Charles I, the new king favored ostentation and loved plays; consequently the theater made a rather quick recovery despite the fact that public playhouses had been pulled down or fallen into disrepair during the Puritan regime.

The spirit of the times had changed, however, and the genial, robust qualities of humanism that had distinguished the theater during the reign of Elizabeth and that had, to a certain extent, persisted into the Jacobean era in the works of Shakespeare and Jonson, had disappeared. Nor was the baroque passion that characterized the tragic plays of the Jacobean playwrights any longer in evidence. Instead, a neoclassic aesthetic—clinging rigorously to a new set of rules that placed great importance on reason, order, and decorum at the expense of emotion and fantasy—was imposed upon playwriting, while literary cliques decided the canons of form, taste, and manners. Passion and verve were supplanted by wit and restraint. Luminaries of the age gathered in coffee and chocolate houses, forerunners of the English club, where gentlemen of quality indulged the "human instinct to retail news and gossip," developing conversation into a cold and dispassionate art.

Two acting companies were licensed in London: the Duke of York's Company, which obtained its charter in 1661, under the direction of the brilliant stage designer-manager Richard Davenant; and the King's Company, which was given its permit in 1663, with Thomas Killigrew as manager. These two companies, with their royal patents, jointly held a monopoly on public theater. Davenant housed his company in Duke's House in Lincoln's Inn Fields while Killigrew's company performed at the Theatre Royal. Interestingly enough, both these royal patents still belong to theaters now in operation: Killigrew's to the Covent Garden Opera House, Davenant's to the Drury Lane.

To answer the new canons of theatrical taste, John Dryden created the heroic play, which attempted "the portrayal on an heroic scale of conflicts in love and mighty deeds." Its main characteristics were rant, bombast, an overcomplicated plot, and an exotic setting. The best example of this short-lived genre is Dryden's *Indian Queen,* produced in 1664. Never very popular, the heroic play was summarily done in by

the Duke of Buckingham's burlesque of the genre, *The Rehearsal*, which appeared in 1671. The successor to the heroic play was a type of tragedy in which the rhymed couplets of the heroic style were abandoned for blank verse, so much more congenial to English. Dryden's greatest achievement in the new form was *All for Love*, a reworking of the story of Antony and Cleopatra.

But it was naturally the comedy of wit and manners that triumphed in the gossipy Restoration period. In the hands of William Wycherly, William Congreve, and George Farquhar, English Restoration comedy achieved genuine brilliance. The genre is marked by hardness and lack of feeling, yet its quick wit and rapier-sharp dialogue have never been excelled in English. How much less distinguished the history of English comedy would be without such delightful plays as Wycherly's *The Country Wife*, Congreve's *Love for Love* and *The Way of the World*, and Farquhar's *The Recruiting Officer*, all produced between the years 1673 and 1706.

Another delight of the Restoration stage was the appearance of actresses, who, without any real training, took over the roles long played on the English stage by boys. Among the most famous was Nell Gwynne, the erstwhile orange seller who became the mistress of Charles II. Several wives of actors, such as Mrs. Betterton, Mrs. Knipp, and Mrs. Bracegirdle, became favorites of the London theatergoers almost as soon as they appeared.

The covered playhouse of the Restoration period was quite different from the open-roofed, octagonal Elizabethan theater. The former consisted of a divided stage, half of which protruded into the audience and half of which lay behind the proscenium arch, shut off from view by a series of folding screens that could be opened to indicate a change of scene. While the greater part of the action took place on the thrust stage in front of the proscenium, the area within the arch was used for

The wit of Restoration drama marked the seventeenth century in England. Women were permitted to play in Colley Cibber's comedy of manners, The Careless Husband (opposite), in which the author himself took the lead. David Garrick, the next century's greatest actor, played women's parts too, and he is shown above costumed as an old woman. Garrick's Drury Lane Theater (left, below) was a London showcase for Shakespearean and Restoration productions for almost twenty years.

94

fantastic scenic effects. Since the roof now closed out the natural light, artificial lighting was used in an increasingly elaborate way. (The first reflector lights were improvised by standing metal shaving bowls behind lamps.) Tiers of separated boxes rose steeply on three sides of the thrust stage, and the old pit was fitted out with seats or benches. At the very top of the house stood the "gallery gods," those who had paid only for general admission.

The audience no longer represented the entire population, as it had in Elizabethan days, for the poor had grown poorer. Theater for them had become an ill-afforded luxury. Moreover, they could scarcely be expected to be interested in the highly artificial picture of life presented in most plays of the period. The theater, a social institution of the wealthy middle class, became a hive of social activity and intrigue, the locus of fashionable cabals and snobbish cliques, a place in which to be seen and talked about.

The late seventeenth and early eighteenth centuries also marked a period of unusually great acting. The legendary David Garrick, joined by Thomas Betterton, John Rich, and Colley Cibber, competed against one another in the whole gamut of tragedy and comedy, sometimes writing their own versions of Shakespeare's plays and tailoring them to fit their own whims or talents. The neoclassic period instituted many significant and enduring theatrical conventions and practices: the proscenium arch, artificial lighting, the complete segregation of the audience by a system of ticket pricing, the institution of rented boxes and loges, realistic scenery, the paid claque, and the hegemony of the theater critic. All, of course, are still in evidence in the theater of today.

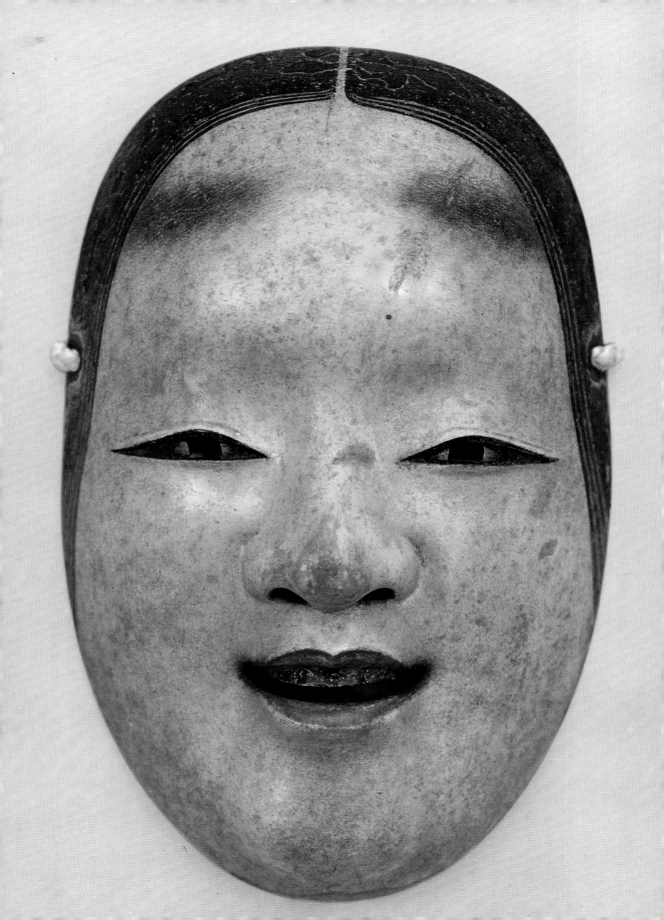

6

Common Roots, Uncommon Forms

THERE IS AN ANCIENT ADAGE which states that, like the daylight, all things begin in the East. This is certainly true of the Indo-European language system, the ancient antecedent of most Western languages, which can be traced back five thousand years to the Indus Valley in the northwest corner of the Indian subcontinent. Although not readily discernible to the untrained ear, this strong linguistic link is revealed in the most elemental thought patterns of Western men—and consequently in their most familiar expressions. It is no surprise, then, that they share the common epithet, "Mother India," which acknowledges the measure and the nature of the West's cultural debt to ancient India.

The "collective imagination" of India has always been rich and active; there the status of the myth has not lost its primitive power, nor has it disappeared into the unconscious as it has in the West. Myths, to the Hindu, are merely one expression of reality—illusions by which man, in his limited way, helps himself to comprehend the vast, incomprehensible universe. The Hindu therefore prefers to consider the phenomenal world not as a battlefield of principles but as a theater for the display of natural forces, created by his divinities.

It can be safely argued that all major Oriental theater forms had their beginnings in India, for even after centuries of growth the initial Indian influences are still discernible in theater forms in China, Korea, and Japan in the north—and in Burma, Thailand, Laos, Cambodia, and Indonesia in the east and south. (Significantly, the ancient Greeks believed that Dionysus, the god of theater, had come to them from the Far East.) India can, then, be called the birthplace of theater, since theater existed in India as an established art at least a thousand years before it was recognized as such elsewhere.

The Indians, like the ancient Greeks, were colonizing traders. Centuries before Buddhist missionaries from India began their successful conversion of Asia, Indian traders had established their trading colonies everywhere in the East, organizing an effective network through which the cultural heritage of India could be easily broadcast. As a result, the foundations of theatrical art and the attitudes toward theater discipline everywhere in the civilized Orient bear a distinctive Indian stamp.

When, in the third century B.C., Buddhist monks began the mammoth task of attempting to win converts outside India, they taught not only the precepts of Siddhartha, Gautama Buddha, but also the

Like commedia dell'arte, the Nō theater of Japan presented stock characters in masks. The mask at left of Ko-omote, the innocent maiden with the "little face," dates to the first half of the sixteenth century. Like aristocratic women of earlier times, she has been depicted with chalk-white makeup, shaved eyebrows, and blackened teeth.

ancient teachings of their five Hindu Vedas and their two ethnic epics, the *Ramayana* and the *Mahabharata*. These epics were to furnish the mythic subjects and themes for theater in all the converted countries. Moreover, the *Natya Sastra*, or fifth Veda, set up exacting rules for theater training and performance. Fortunately for theatrical history, the *Natya Sastra*, until then an oral teaching, was set down in Sanskrit by the prophet-patriarch Bharata toward the beginning of the Christian era, and it can be studied today. Besides laying down the rules for the construction of the playing area, this extraordinary "theater Veda" outlines the seven-year apprenticeship of the actor and the intricate details of his education. It also stipulates that performance must be completely controlled and never impulsive or original in execution. Since the actor must play the roles of gods and heroes, he must achieve perfect art through selfless discipline.

Indian acting and dance are covered by the same expression, *Natya*; consequently, every gesture used by the actor has been choreographed. The *Natya Sastra* rules that the action, not the actor, is the essential attitude in performance—and during his long apprenticeship the postulant is carefully taught this attitude by master performers whose daily rounds of duty are largely devoted to the teaching of students. With no realistic properties and little or no scenery to assist him, the Indian actor must arouse specific emotional reaction in his audience. His art is provocative rather than literal and realistic, and his audience is expected to use its mythic imagination to create the drama's setting. The performing area itself is little more than a square area set off by a border from the spectators, but it is nonetheless considered a sacred precinct. and upon entering it the performer invokes the deity.

Because every particular of Indian drama is regulated by tradition—the stories are all known; the songs, dances, and gestures are always the same—every spectator is able to judge the excellence of the performance for himself. Drama has been a part of his cultural experience from earliest childhood, and consequently he is capable of discussing the relative merits of the execution of the *mudras* ("gestures"), the stage presence of the actors, and the *rasa* ("flavor") of the artist's work.

Ritualized choreography, a part of Indian religious spectacle, was traditionally assigned to apsarases, the dancing women depicted on the bas-relief at left, above. Smooth and sensuous Kathak dancers are portrayed in the miniature opposite. In the middle area, musicians play for dancers whose movements dramatize episodes in the life of Lord Krishna. Around them can be seen vignettes of life at the sixteenth-century court of the Mogul emperor Akbar.

India has produced four great schools of traditional theater, all of which exist today thanks largely to the efforts of India's great nationalist poet Rabindranath Tagore (1861-1941). Two of them, Kathakali and Bharata Natyam, are indigenous to the south; two others, Kathak and Manipuri, belong to the north. Kathakali is a flamboyant, virile version of the epic that requires intricately applied makeup, heavy, skirted costumes, and bejewelled headpieces. It features monsters and demons along with the epic heroes, and it specializes in battles. As could be expected, Kathakali relies exclusively upon male actors, and as a result all the female roles are taken by young men. It is the only Indian theater that requires a curtain, and that curtain bears little resemblance to the curtains used in Western theaters. It is, rather, a richly adorned property that is held up at the beginning of each performance so that the principal actor, about to begin his entrance dance, may peer over it to announce his presence. (Sometimes this curtain serves as a stylized boat, rising and falling with the actor.) Kathakali is performed to an incessant drumming, and the actors' voices are supplied by a narrator. India's other southern theatrical form is Bharata Natyam, which is typical of Madras. In contrast to Kathakali, Bharata Natyam is subtle and feminine, a descendant of the early temple dances traditionally performed by women. As the name implies, the style adheres strictly to the dictates of Bharata, author of the theater Veda.

Kathak is a sensuous style which, although it goes back to ancient Hindu sources, survived the Moslem invasion. It is excessively intricate in its strictly regulated serial rhythms and movements. It is performed by both men and women, although the latter currently outnumber the former. The Manipuri style, associated with Manipur, the Indian province nearest Burma, is famous for its delicate excellence. Unlike other forms of Indian theater it moves in a swaying motion without abrupt breaks or angularity. Rather than celebrating the epics, it dramatizes episodes in the life of Lord Krishna. Particular to Manipur is the Ras Lila, a kind of opera in which dancing, singing, and music are beautifully combined. The fluid quality of these dance-dramas has found its way into the dance-dramas of Thailand and faraway Bali.

During the British occupation of India, ancient theater forms began to decline. Indeed, they might have disappeared altogether had nationalistic amateurs not held fast and refused to let the old forms die out. When India became independent, the state, eager to save its national heritage, helped to revive the four regional styles by granting subsidies to properly constituted centers of instruction. Then in the 1930's, Uday Shankar made the outside world aware of the excellence of Indian theatrical traditions, chiefly by interesting such influential persons as Gordon Craig and Ruth St. Denis in researching the Indian theater. (It was an interest that both Ananda Coomeraswamy, then curator of the Boston Museum, and Professor Raghavan of the University of Madras were capable of sustaining in foreigners.) As a result there exists today a fabulous body of authoritative sources for researching India's ancient theatrical forms, where as a hundred years ago those traditions were close to dying out altogether.

Like ancient Indian theater, Chinese drama has its beginnings in religious rites involving processions of effigies, dancing, singing, and pantomime acts. Not until the sixth century A.D., the cultural apogee of the T'ang dynasty, were the elements of text, song, dance, and comedy combined in a single presentation. These dramatizations commonly involved two men—one playing the role of a drunken husband, the other his mistreated wife. Their hilarious antics were performed inside a chalk circle, and the spectators, who stood around the periphery, sang familiar refrains between the episodes. This early rough-and-tumble form of marketplace entertainment already possessed the features that were to distinguish the eighteenth-century Peking Opera: a simple storyline, capable of being extended and embellished, and two distinct leading roles, each with a set of characteristic stances, gestures, and movements. The play was sung and danced, but there was also spoken dialogue and orchestral accompaniment. The acting consisted largely of mimed gestures, and the plays themselves were presented out of doors.

With the aid of her long sleeves and elegantly balanced stance, the T'ang dynasty dancing girl reproduced in terracotta at left, above, appears especially graceful in comparison with the rigid lines of the Malay shadow puppet at left, below. At right, a dancer from China's Peking Opera leads the lion character so popular in theatrical productions of the Far East.

Overleaf: *Male and female characters of the Peking Opera strike stylized poses.*

Unlike Indian theater, which set up a sacred precinct for all performances, Chinese theater–always much more secular in its Taoist attitudes–used only the conventional chalk circle to designate the performing area. For centuries, therefore, it was possible to set up a playing space anywhere merely by drawing a circle on the ground. Actors quickly learned to assume a given character when entering the circle—only to drop it when they left it. This famous in-and-out convention, which seems always to have been a distinctive characteristic of Chinese theater, fascinated the twentieth-century German playwright Bertolt Brecht, who incorporated it into the acting technique of his epic theater. Brecht also favored a highly episodic dramatic structure, breaking the flow of the action with songs and narration in a manner that was traditionally Chinese.

The Chinese, like the Indians, have never really subscribed to the notion of realistic settings or properties. Although both theater traditions insist upon elaborate costumes, headpieces, and makeup, both rely upon the evocative talents of the actors and the imaginations of the spectators to localize the action of the plays. While both make use of symbolic properties, Chinese theater also includes a few simple props such as tables and chairs, which might serve as stairs, mountains, thrones—whatever the story requires.

Throughout their history, Chinese actors have been experts at illusionism, creating the impression of a vast, magic world through their astounding mastery of physical dexterity. In one scene, ferrymen pole their boats across imaginary rivers as they battle their way through the rapids, their squeamish lady passengers protesting in perfect coordination. In another, a lady chases an imaginary butterfly, climbs an imaginary ladder to pluck an imaginary flower, teeters, almost loses her balance, and rights herself.

The Indian influences on Chinese theater, brought to China two centuries before the Christian era, can still be seen in the harsh, demanding apprenticeship for actors that traditionally lasts for seven years. Rigorously imposed by master teachers who are the watchdogs of style in gesture, movement, and vocal expression, this apprenticeship regulates every phase of the aspirant's progress until after he has graduated to the rank of beginning actor.

The renowned Peking Opera represents the very best in Chinese theater tradition. Its texts, by no means extraordinary as literary pieces, are mere pretexts for virtuosity in acting, singing, declamation, mime, and acrobatics. Lyric scenes alternate with splendid battle interludes in which the performers display their amazing skills; fantastic lions caper, circle, and challenge each other, disappearing with gigantic leaps; warriors, mounted on imaginary steeds, wheel and attack, veer and retreat. The actors specialize in one of four main types of roles: Cheng, the designation for the young leading man, the warrior, or the bearded patriarch; Tan, the serious young woman, the frivolous maiden, the amazon, or the crone; Tsing—literally a "painted face"—one of the many legendary character roles requiring elaborate, stylized makeup; and Tch'eou or Tch'eon-tan, comic roles.

Women were forbidden by decree to appear on stage in China, and consequently Tan roles became a specialty of many Chinese actors. The greatest of contemporary Tan specialists is Mei Lan Fang, who performed the roles of courtesans and maidens until he was in his seventies. The proscription against women has been lifted in present-day China, and the superb training of the Peking Opera, once confined to the capital, has now been made available in new training centers throughout China. Predominantly didactic and moralizing, the Peking Opera's repertory has been adopted as a teaching device in China today, and many new pieces, patterned on old familiar plays, have now replaced less relevant ones.

Since well before the Christian era, China has maintained a well-defined tradition of puppetry and shadow plays. This tradition of animated dolls and ornate shadow cutouts, which was once considered

rude folk art, later developed into the refined shadow-puppet shows of the court, played from tiny boat-theaters in the lily ponds of the palace gardens. The Chinese government recently rescued these disappearing forms from threatened oblivion, and it is now subsidizing their continuation in regional centers. Once thought of as childish amusements they have now become instructional media in many of the government's reform projects, particularly in rural areas.

No country in the world has so continuously and so carefully preserved its theater traditions as Japan. When the first Buddhist missionaries arrived in that island empire during the early Christian era, they found a well-established tradition of ritual dances connected with Shinto, the ancient national religion. These missionaries taught their converts certain masked dances from India and instructed them in Sanskrit teachings of the Vedas regarding such performances. Later, in the seventh century, when the Chinese were enjoying a period of great influence at the Japanese court, another group of dances from the mainland was adopted. Many of these dances—including the Japanese forms called Gigaku and later Chinese and Korean additions known as Bugaku—are performed in Japan today. Gigaku performances have a legendary connection with the mythic beginning of dance and music in Japan, and such dances are still performed at temples throughout the country during festival time. Bugaku, maintained as a ritual entertainment at court and, until recent years, rarely seen by those not intimately attached to the imperial household or the diplomatic service, still preserves that angularity and sharpness of movement that are so characteristic of Indian dances and so unlike the slow, undulating, legato movements of typically Japanese dances. Moreover, the patterns of Bugaku are not only symmetrical but also extremely complicated, weaving in and out from the center and producing an almost hypnotic effect. At times Bugaku employs both masks and bits of Sanskrit texts, indications of its distant Indian origin. These ancient dance forms must have been representational at one time, but they are now highly abstract and geometrical in form and movement.

If the Japanese have shown a predilection for solemn ceremoniousness in their performances, they have also demonstrated a great fond-

A woman of the Peking Opera (left) enacts a legendary character in elaborate dress. The ancient Nō theater is one of mime and ritual movement; the Nō actor above wears a "little face" mask representing freshness and purity. Kabuki theater involves more plot and conversation; modern Kabuki actors appear below on a Tokyo stage.

ness for the comic, the erotic, and the obscene. There is no denying, for example, that the oldest myth explaining the origin of theater in Japan has its comic, erotic, and obscene sides. According to that tale the goddess Ama-no-Uzume-no-Mikoto, in order to trick her sister the sun goddess into coming out of a cave where she was hiding, performed a half-naked dance on a sounding board before the blocked-up mouth of the cave. So comic and obscene was this dance that all the other gods screamed with laughter, and the sun, dying of curiosity, peeped out—and thereby illuminated the dark world. This tradition of satirical obscenity and eroticism is also evident in Sarugaku, the mimed interludes that were popular in Prince Genji's day and are still performed at popular gatherings.

A considerable repertory of dances has been preserved from the Dengaku, or rural folk dances that celebrate the harvest. These have their place in the liturgical calendar of Shinto, but a number have found their way into both Nō and Kabuki plays. Of the three main types of performances in Japan—Nō, Jōruri, and Kabuki—Nō is by many centuries the oldest and most refined. It is both the oldest living drama of any importance in the world today and the only one that still employs masks.

Nō was certainly in existence several hundred years before the actor Kanami, and his son Seami, formalized it in the late fourteenth century.

For centuries the eclectic style of the Kabuki theater has been fully ritualized. For instance, the actor Otani Oniji (right) underwent a seven-year apprenticeship in the 1700's—just as Kabuki actors do today. Below, in a woodblock print by Utagawa Toyokuni, an eighteenth-century Kabuki group performs.

At the time there existed two distinct forms of dance-drama—Dengaku-no-Nō, an admixture of dance and exquisitely expressed literary texts, and Sarugaku-no-Nō, gross farces and grotesque demon dances. The two forms were rivals. Under the sponsorship of Ashikaga Yoshimitsu, a young and powerful shogun, Kanami and his son established the rules for Nō. So well instituted were their regulations that five centuries later, when the long-lost written record of the "secret tradition" was rediscovered, the training and performance were still virtually identical to what they had been when they were first written down in the fifteenth century. Indeed, every detail of Nō is deliberately calculated—the exact size of the stage, with its four-pillared roof and its long *hashigakari*, or entrance ramp; the places assigned to the chorus and the musicians; the three small pine trees that always border the passageway; the unchanging painted backdrop; and the actors' elegant costumes and impassive masks.

Nō plays are divided into five categories according to subject: god plays, warrior-ghost plays, insanity plays of revenge, love-story plays, and demon plays. It is customary to perform the entire five-part series preceded by the *okina*, a dance depicting the three ages of man. Such performances often strike Westerners as tedious, for their theatrical heritage is derived from the Greek principle of active conflict. In Nō there is no action in the Western sense; instead, everything in a Nō play has already happened and is being recalled. The principal actor, called the *shite*, and his foil, the second actor, or *waki*, are the oldest and the only essential actors in a Nō play, although each of these may have an attendant or two called *tsure*. There may also be a comic who enters to present another set of considerations to the attention of the audience. (It is interesting to note that each of these two principals and their attendants go to different schools for their training.) The principal actors often wear blind masks, a feat that causes them no consternation, since they must know the exact number of steps, turns, and positions in each role.

Among the many varieties of Sarugaku popular in Japan during the thirteenth century was a simple form that consisted solely of a wandering monk who sang long pseudoepics while accompanying himself on the biwa, a four-stringed lute. The most popular of the song cycles sung in these heike-biwa recitations was that concerning the maiden Jōruri and a samurai warrior of the Minamoto clan. This song's twelve episodes grew so familiar that they became known as the Jōruri—and through extended use the term Jōruri came to designate the manner of reciting it to music. The biwa was replaced by the more expressive shamisen—a kind of three-stringed guitar that has been the favorite instrument of all Jōruri artists since the fourteenth century.

By the end of the seventeenth century there were Jōruri schools in Kyoto, Osaka, and Tokyo. The texts they used were largely invented by the chanters themselves, and although they were rich and varied they tended to be of poor literary quality. An ancient rural custom of illustrating the recitations of poems with crude dolls of wood or clay was adopted toward the middle of the seventeenth century by the Jōruri school of Osaka, and with that Ningyo-jōruri—Jōruri with dolls

—was created. In 1684, the Jōruri artist Takemoto Gidayo opened the Takemoto-za in Osaka, a theater exclusively for the performance of Jōruri. He quickly recognized that his venture could not hope to succeed in attracting a desirable audience without excellently crafted plays, and he addressed himself to Chikamatsu Monzaemon, a playwright who until then had written plays for Kabuki. Chikamatsu, known as the Shakespeare of Japan, was a literary genius who immediately understood the artistic and dramatic potential of the Ningyo-jōruri, and he wrote for the performers of the Takemoto-za for close to forty years. Under the artistic direction of Gidayo–and armed with a dramatic arsenal written by Chikamatsu–the troupe at the Takemoto-za became one of the three major branches of Japanese theater. Internationally known through its many tours abroad, this troupe has not only insured the survival of the magnificent art of Jōruri—or Bunraku, as it is more generally known—it has brought the art of puppetry to unsurpassed heights. The perfectly coordinated workings of these exquisitely fashioned dolls, each of which requires three operators; the astonishingly varied vocal patterns of the Jōruri performers; and the restrained, subtly dramatic accompaniment of the shamisen players all contribute with equal artistry to create Bunraku—one of the great treasures of world theater.

Of the three great divisions of Japanese theater–Nō, Jōruri, and Kabuki—the last is without doubt the most popular. Like both Nō and Jōruri, Kabuki is a descendant of ancient Sarugaku performances. In the early years of the seventeenth century, O-Kuni, an erotic dancer of extraordinary talents, invented a sensational type of dance-drama that required a large troupe of performers. She became the toast of her day, and after her death others assumed the direction of the troupe she had formed. In time the so-called Pleasure Woman's Kabuki became so notorious for its immorality that all women were forbidden by official ban to perform in public. After 1630 women's roles were taken by young boys, but still greater scandal ensued and twenty-two years later they too were put under interdiction. Certain Kyogen actors—the clowns of Japanese theater—then left off playing their usually ribald roles and took the women's parts, developing the delicate onnagata style that is such an admired feature of modern Kabuki. With two able rivals—No and the puppet theater—Kabuki was forced to incorporate elements from both. In fact, the puppeteers became so popular after Chikamatsu began to write for them that Kabuki actors found reasons to copy religiously the style of the puppets and perform many of the plays Chikamatsu had written for the Jōruri. Kabuki thus became a living anthology of Japanese theater, where, in the course of a performance, one might see dances from every past age; staged battles; tiny, evocative mood pieces; acts of *seppuku*, or ritual suicide; fearsome appearances in aragoto style, the dramatic behavior of supermen; passages of Jōruri; and lion dances. Kabuki is full of surprises—scenic effects of the most splendid sort are one of its specialties—and because of this spectacular array of talent, Kabuki requires long, arduous training in which every detail of artistry is patiently assumed. Actors begin their training at the age of five, inheriting their right to study from

Kabuki actors such as the one below consider themselves students of thousands of specific movements and situations. Bunraku puppets, one of which is seen opposite, are also capable of a wide range of expressions.

their actor fathers. The *kata*—rules and traditions of Kabuki acting—must be completely mastered, and no originality is tolerated. Thus Kabuki, which began in disrepute, is now a respected repository of Japanese culture, a kind of living history of Japanese theater. Its actors, respected artists, are often decorated by the government for their dedication to a most difficult and obliging art.

In summing up the most salient differences between the theater of the Orient and that of the West, one is struck by the powerful, continued use of the collective imagination in the East; in the theater of the West what little use of the imagination ancient Greek and Elizabethan theater demanded was soon supplanted by an ever-increasing desire for realism. This supposed proximity of art and everyday reality in Western aesthetics has led to the popular belief that actors simply act out their real, everyday experiences and consequently require little training. This is the contrary of ancient, deep-seated attitudes toward actors' training in the Orient where, following an almost absolute directive from ancient Indian sources, actors must train for a minimum of seven years before they are allowed to appear in a public performance. The Oriental answer to the Western actor's prejudice against too much technical training in acting is that only through supreme control of technique is one liberated from it, an attitude that expresses the radical difference between the theater of the Orient and that of the West. Ironically enough, it is just this cardinal difference in attitude that accounts for the rich variety of Oriental theater forms and the near homogeneity of Western theater forms.

7

The Rise of Romanticism

Three men clasp hands and vow allegiance to one another and to their romantic vision of a free and democratic Switzerland. The play is Johann Schiller's Wilhelm Tell; the performance is in Hamburg, Germany; the time, 1804. The spirit is that of triumphant, heroic action—post-dating the French Revolution and predating German attempts to duplicate that revolution.

BY THE MIDDLE of the eighteenth century, France had attained far greater intellectual and artistic stature in Western Europe and the New World than Cardinal Richelieu had dreamed possible. Louis XIII's powerful adviser had envisioned French culture as a dominant civilizing force in world affairs, but even he had failed to predict the scope and direction of that thrust. The prestigious *présence française*—for which both Richelieu and Mazarin had labored—did not produce an enlightened, classical elitist aristocracy, as the prelates had hoped; rather, with unprecedented thoroughness and dispatch it supplied waiting minds everywhere with the tools of radical democratization.

Ironically, the galvanic impact of the *présence française* would never have occurred had it not been nurtured in its formative stages by certain well-established agencies of the period, in particular the French academies, for which both cardinals, by their patronage, were in some measure responsible. For example, it was the academies, with their intellectual interests in science, history, and philosophy—and with their progressivist views on education—that encouraged the efforts of Denis Diderot and the Encyclopedists. And it was the *philosophes* of the Age of Reason, in turn, who provided the instrumentation for the democratization of education by compiling universal knowledge in a comprehensive form under a simple alphabetical system.

The other great democratizing force at work in eighteenth-century France was the newspaper. As a scholarly forum for the dissemination of recent scientific discoveries, the debate of social issues, and the enunciation of radical philosophies, these newspapers were without precedent or peer, and as a result they attracted the greatest minds of the age. Jean Jacques Rousseau, for example, wrote both the *Discourse on the Sciences and Arts* and the *Discourse on the Origin of Inequality* for essay contests sponsored by the Academy of Dijon through the *Mercure de France*.

Largely through the encyclopedia and the newspaper, those two surrogates for real experience, France in the mid-1700's became the perfect reflection of ideal social, political, and cultural fashion for literate men everywhere. The humanistic idealism of fundamental Neoplatonism—which had been present at the inception of the Italian Renaissance and which had, almost entirely unnoticed, accompanied its subsequent growth—now sprang forth everywhere with the strength of a natural reflex. The reintroduction of this philosophy through the popular literature of the day gave rise to the widespread belief that the world was experiencing the spontaneous manifestation of some mysterious *Zeitgeist*. The German philosopher Ernst Cassirer has pointed out that there was, in fact, a widespread belief that original, spontaneous thought could and should be considered not merely as an imitative function but also as a power capable of shaping life itself.

This belief in a progressive, democratic "spirit of the times"—in contrast to a conservative, aristocratic, socially imposed order—prepared the intellectual climate for romanticism, the most revolutionary aesthetic yet to appear in European history. In its passionate acceptance of the superiority of free, subjective reality, romanticism sought absolute freedom from the conventional constraints of society, which were held to be corrupting rather than correcting forces in individual lives. The true romantic saw himself as a lonely hero pitted against an evil society, with only his "natural" sentiments to restrain and guide him. For such a man, conflict with the opposing forces of society became a natural obligation, a matter of conscience. Not surprisingly, this new philosophy of social revolution, with its belief in conflict, quickly discovered in the theater a forceful and congenial medium for disseminating its views.

At its most altruistic, romanticism in the theater allied itself with the late-eighteenth- and early-nineteenth-century struggles for social and political equality, producing dramas such as the German poet-playwright Johann Schiller's *Wilhelm Tell*; at its most subjective, it provided an aesthetic of paranoia, of which Georg Büchner's *Woyzeck* is a good example. The degree to which romanticism of any cast differed from all antecedent aesthetics is perhaps best demonstrated by tracing the history of a famed theatrical archetype, the wily servant, through the main steps of his development. In the plays of Plautus, written more than two thousand years ago, the crafty slave Maccus was depicted as just clever enough to dupe his dull-witted master and his gullible fellow slaves. Arlecchino, the fast-talking servant of the Italian commedia dell' arte, was shown to be a shade more clever than his generic ancestor, Maccus, but he was seldom depicted as truly intelligent. He might, for instance, cast fleers at his bourgeois master, Pantelone, but these were satiric attacks upon personal quirks rather than class foibles. (Indeed, there was not so much as a hint of social criticism in the commedia dell'arte.) With the seventeenth-century Spanish picaroon, of whom Clarín in Calderón's greatest drama, *Life Is a Dream*, is typical, mere cleverness began to give way to real intelligence, and these classless rogues often pointed out that stupidity was not the exclusive possession of any one class or profession.

Molière, for his part, gave his plucky servants common sense, and he often allowed them to chide the bourgeois households of their masters for allowing a set of modish affectations and circumstances to stifle natural sense and obscure the truth. Carrying this trend a step farther, the eponymous hero of Pierre Beaumarchais' *The Marriage of Figaro* was to condemn the immorality of the entire nobility. Calling the social order of the late eighteenth century to task, the playwright was ques-

In The Barber of Seville, *written in 1772, Pierre Beaumarchais viewed the question of social change as a struggle of individuals, but in* The Marriage of Figaro, *completed twelve years later, he found fault with the whole structure of society. The well-composed eighteenth-century watercolor above, which depicts Louise Contat posing as the cunning character Susanna in the second Beaumarchais play, admits no prescience of the bloodshed to begin in 1789. At right are the gay performers of Goya's* Los comicos ambulantes.

tioning the concept of inherited, and often unmerited, superiority.

In a sense the romantics' attack on the neoclassic aesthetic in theater was nothing more than a logical extension of the sweeping social changes that had been spawned by the French Revolution. The same spirit of criticism that had led Beaumarchais' Figaro to question the legitimacy of the established social order now led dramatists and critics alike to question the legitimacy of certain long-accepted attitudes concerning the nature of theater.

In Germany, Gotthold Ephraim Lessing was the first to reject the influence of French classicism—which he had experienced firsthand during a brief period in his youth when he undertook translations for the aging Voltaire. The two men soon quarreled and parted, Lessing to create the very *tragédies bourgeois* that Voltaire had pontificated against. Postulating a return to the informal style of Shakespeare, Lessing created *Minna von Barnhelm*, Germany's first contemporary drama, in 1767. Slightly more than a decade later he published his acknowledged masterpiece, *Nathan the Wise*, which introduced blank verse to the German stage. In the interim, Lessing was to produce a body of

critical work that has assumed far greater significance than his plays. From 1767 to 1768 he exerted considerable aesthetic influence as the official artistic director and critic of an important dramatic company in Hamburg, where he and the well-known actor Ernst Ackermann tried to set up a national theater. Their venture was doomed to failure for a number of reasons, but the experiment they conducted was a towering success. Before it had run its course Lessing had made a careful, critical examination of playwriting, acting, and theater management. Under the collective title *Hamburg Dramaturgy*, these observations and recommendations were to become the basis for German theatrical practice.

The romantic movement found strong support in another German playwright, Johann Schiller, who wrote one fine play after another during the closing decades of the eighteenth century, a period when Germany was blessed with the most dynamic and innovative playwrights to be found anywhere in the world. This development is all the more remarkable in light of the fact that German theater of the early eighteenth century was nothing less than a national embarrassment. Rehearsals, memorization of lines, effective scenery, and inventive staging were virtually nonexistent, and theater, such as it was, consisted of low harlequinades—known by the name of their principal figure, the

France's revolutionary spirit was reflected in Gotthold Lessing's classical drama Minna von Barnhelm, *a story of "real people"—a woman and an officer in the Prussian army. A scene from that 1763 play is shown above. Historical themes were the basis for many of Schiller's plays, and the painting at left, from a performance of his* Maid of Orleans, *shows Frenchmen awaiting the coronation of Charles VII, Joan's dauphin. In the Paris of the 1830's, republicans cheered Victor Hugo's romantic and lyrical* Hernani *and its Robin Hood-like hero while classicists hissed—as the view opposite of opening night indicates.*

Overleaf: *Some doze, some peer, some talk or stare in Honoré Daumier's satirical view of mid-nineteenth-century French theatergoers,* L'entr'acte.

buffoon Hanswurst—that were little more than coarse improvisation upon an open platform.

Thanks largely to Lessing and a handful of reform-minded acting troupes, German theater underwent a remarkable metamorphosis during the latter half of the century. Schiller's *The Maid of Orleans*, *Don Carlos*, and *Wilhelm Tell*, all championing the individual against conventional oppression and all products of this theatrical renaissance, were received with great enthusiasm by the young writers of the *Sturm und Drang* movement, writers who were already making known their passionate espousal of the absolute rights of individual genius.

In rapid order the new spirit of revolt spread throughout Europe, manifesting itself on stages everywhere. Russia's first and greatest poet, Alexander Pushkin, wrote his revolutionary *Boris Godunov* in 1825, and the great Nikolai Gogol produced his biting satire *The Inspector General* in 1836. Both plays demonstrate the far-reaching effects of the romantic movement, although both are colored by the theme of submission to the environment, a peculiarly Russian quality. In Paris, France's greatest poet, Victor Hugo, announced his romantic credo in *Cromwell*, an unacted–and perhaps unactable–verse drama, in 1827. Because of its great length the play was never produced, but its preface was accepted by the French romantics as a battle cry for the violent overthrow of French conservatism and its neoclassic aesthetic. Three years later, the opening night of Hugo's *Hernani* at the Comédie

Française was the occasion of a riot in that sedate theater. When the conservative neoclassicists in the audience began to taunt the players with cries of "Racine!" the poet and novelist Théophile Gautier jumped to his feet and shouted "Your Racine is a rascal!"—and the battle was joined.

One of the democratizing effects of romanticism was the return of the masses to the theater. No longer the preserve of the privileged and the "precious," theater now addressed itself to the natural, universal, and sentimental—and the standees and "gallery gods" returned to shout their approval or disapproval of the plays and the performances. For theater managers it was a period of profit, and new playhouses were provided for the newly won public. Special seats were often set on the stage itself, and while these prize seats were an excellent source of income for the managers, they represented a real hazard for the actors and a nuisance for the rest of the audience. In England, rakish young lords and their toadies, seated on the stage, often engaged in rude exchanges with the actors and the audience. There were, in fact, so many disruptions that the reading of the Riot Act by London's leading actors became a common occurrence.

Much to the consternation of actors and managers everywhere, a general relaxation of conventional public behavior followed the widespread acceptance of the tenets of romanticism. Even after the practice of seating spectators on the stage had been abandoned, disputes and fights in the theater remained so common that in most countries public laws provided that police officers be present at every performance.

In Germany in this period, Johann Wolfgang von Goethe was to initiate a systematic examination of dramatic art, studying the problems of directing, acting, playwriting, and production. Like Lessing, Goethe's criticism was sharper than his self-criticism, and even the playwright's later greatest works—a list headed by the extraordinary *Faust*, pinnacle of German tragic drama—are distressingly amorphous. In the case of *Egmont*, an idyllic depiction of love in time of war, this formlessness can be attributed to a willing subjugation of style to subject matter. In the more critical and more intriguing case of *Faust*, this lack of pure theatricality must be ascribed, at least in part, to the fact that Goethe reworked his masterpiece for more than half a century—from 1775 until his death in 1832. Indeed, the second half of the play, a paean to the "wondrous workings of civilization," was published shortly after the playwright's death.

A sixteenth-century conjurer and entertainer became linked with medieval legends of men in league with the devil, and numerous artistic productions concerning the aspiring Faust resulted. The best and most romantic of these is Johann Wolfgang von Goethe's dramatic poem Faust. *In a painting by Ludwig von Carosfeld, Faust visits Marguerite in prison.*

As both critic and author, Goethe favored a classic attitude over a romantic one. "First the beautiful, then the true to life!" he exclaimed, disagreeing with the actor, theater manager, and playwright Friedrich Schröder, who had instituted a more realistic attitude toward theater practice. Thanks to Goethe and Schröder's proselytizing—and to the enlightened attitudes of the courts at Weimar, Berlin, and Vienna—early-nineteenth-century German theater was given an honored place in cultural and educational considerations. Out of this concern was to grow a system of national and municipal subsidies for the theater that assured popular drama a more secure position in Germany and Austria than in any other European countries.

Acting came into its own during the romantic period, when leading actors of both the French and English stages advocated modifying the declamatory style in the direction of normal speech. At left, France's François Talma in the part of Hamlet, with a Mlle. Duchesnois as Gertrude. Above is a clown painted by J. A. Watteau.

No sooner had the revolutionary romantics discovered that theater was an effective means of making their liberal views known to a wide audience than the conservative forces of the establishment also recognized drama's political potential. Licensing ordinances, laws of public safety designed to limit the sale of tickets and regulate seating arrangements, and orders of censorship were instituted across the Continent. Meanwhile, organized religion, recognizing an adversary in the rebellious spirit of the romantics, exerted afresh its opposition to theater.

Concomitant with the rise of romanticism came an intense interest in the art of acting. Goethe and Lessing had not only given considerable attention to the specifics of what they meant when they spoke of excellent acting, they had also suggested how an actor ought to be educated and trained in his art. In doing so they had disagreed with Schreyvogel's Viennese school of "acting from within," their dissension marking the beginnings of the "classic" versus "method" acting controversies of our own day. Diderot himself made a valuable contribution to the investigation of the art with his *Paradox of the Actor*, an insightful dialogue on the psychology of the thespian.

Great actors abounded in the romantic period. In England, the peerless David Garrick continued to captivate audiences with his performances of self-tailored Shakespearean roles, and for almost half a century Sarah Siddons, "the Tragic Muse," reigned supreme on the English stage, the darling of such distinguished gentlemen as Dr. Samuel Johnson, Horace Walpole, and the painters Reynolds, Lawrence, and Gainsborough. In France, François Talma was not only preeminent as an actor, but with the help of his friend the painter Jacques Louis David, he initiated a reform in the costuming of French classical plays, adopting designs that were at once easier to manage and more historically correct.

Pantomime, on the wane since the disappearance of the Italian troupes, made a strong reappearance both in London and Paris. At the Drury Lane, Joseph Grimaldi drew enormous crowds to the theater with his creation "Clown," the only really English character in the Christmas Harlequinades—which were otherwise drawn exclusively from characters developed by the commedia dell'arte. Grimaldi was a brilliant improvisor in pantomime, acrobatics, song, and dance, and he completely won over the hearts of the London crowds. In Paris, Jean-Gaspard Deburau, Grimaldi's French counterpart, played openly to the galleries of the Funambules Theatre with his pantomimes of the lovesick Pierrot. True creatures of the romantic period, Grimaldi and Deburau may be said to have represented the nonpolitical, sentimental, and human extremes of the romantic spectrum.

8

A New Theater
for a New Audience

During the late nineteenth century, the energy that had earlier supported romanticism flowed into realism, culminating in the zeal for objective detail expressed in the works of Émile Zola. His plays presented the lives of nonheroic people in mundane environments, as depicted in Théophile Steinlen's turn-of-the-century poster for Zola's successfully dramatized novel L'Assommoir.

INTERESTINGLY ENOUGH, two of the greatest figures of the Age of Enlightenment, the *philosophes* Diderot and Voltaire, were among those responsible for the propagation of bourgeois theater in eighteenth-century France. Members of the middle class, whose patronage had become the legitimate theater's principal source of revenue, were demanding to see their own lives, values, and problems represented on stage. Theirs was a largely materialistic, work-a-day world, prosperous but hardly profound, and it clearly deserved theatrical representation. At times it also plainly invited satirization—and particularly during the middle decades of the century Diderot and Voltaire seemed inclined to give the middle class both.

These French writers, famous for their excellent contributions to theater criticism and for their speculations concerning acting, playwriting, and the aesthetics of theater, wrote sentimental, moralistic plays. These works have not borne up well in comparison with their scholarly works—and certainly not with the best plays of such contemporaries as Pierre Marivaux—but they did have a very strong appeal for middle-class audiences across Europe. It is clear from the success of Diderot's plays in particular that such audiences wanted to laugh at their foibles, but that strong convictions about respectability demanded tears as well. For them, Diderot created the so-called *comédie larmoyante*, or "tearful comedy," with such plays as *The Father of a Family*, performed in 1761, and *The Illegitimate Son*, staged ten years later. The titles are self-explanatory: these were sentimental melodramas that touched the domestic sensibilities of the bourgeoisie, raising fundamental questions regarding natural rights, social injustice, and self-sacrifice. They also sensibly provided everyday dialogue and a happy ending, thus satisfying a large segment of the audience and taking the first step toward realism in theater—a hundred years before Émile Zola and Henrik Ibsen.

Throughout this period and well into the next century, conservative elements dominated most state theaters, a situation reflected both in the choice of plays—mostly classical—and in the production style, which favored traditional settings and sought to bolster national pride with shows of official opulence. But here too the forces of democratization were at work—and nowhere were the political and aesthetic battlelines between conservative and liberal viewpoints drawn more emphatically than in late-nineteenth-century Paris. After a series of political disasters

involving the loss of the Sudan, war with Prussia, and the rise and fall of the 1871 Commune, the resilient Parisians had celebrated the restoration of civil equilibrium by underwriting the cost of constructing the Opéra, on which the designer, Jean Louis Charles Garnier, lavished every embellishment. The new Opéra, along with the state-subsidized Opéra-Comique and the Comédie Française, became the official artistic stronghold of the empire during the Belle Epoque. In the official view, theater served the national purpose as a showcase for French culture and affluence, and as a result, established classics alternated at the Opéra with the works of such officially accepted composers as Georges Bizet, Jules Massenet, and Camille Saint-Saëns. The Dumas, père et fils, Emile Augier, and Victorien Sardou, whose sentimental moralizing gave a specious sense of depth to the government officials, military officers, and bureaucrats who peopled their plays, were also favored with state-supported productions.

Memories of the black days of the Commune and fear of welling socialism provided the rationale and the emotional impetus for rigid government censorship of all theatrical works during the Belle Epoque. Regulation meant vitiation, at least on a thematic level, and emphasis soon shifted from philosophical content to plot and technique. As a result, the ruling class of the empire found itself patronizing boulevard theaters where Eugène Scribe and later Georges Feydeau provided superbly crafted but essentially frivolous domestic farces for their entertainment. Parisians of the period also flocked to the Boulevard du Temple, nicknamed the "Boulevard du Crime," to see terrifying melodramas by the prolific Guilbert de Pixérécourt, whose productions were to impress three generations of English children in the form of the "penny plain, two-pence coloured" theater cutouts sold in English toy shops. It is, however, the works of Jacques Offenbach and his librettists, Nehri Meilhac and Ludovic Halévy, that provide us with the most accurate impression of the theatrical tastes of the haute bourgeoisie, for Offenbach's team was to achieve stunning success with a succession of domesticated myths and exotic tales served up with gay Viennese waltzes and cancans.

While the upper stratum of Parisian society was amusing itself at Offenbach's tiny Bonbonnière and along the Boulevard du Crime, those

Mon Dieu qui me la rens me la rens-tu chrétienne ?

Realistic drama had its roots in the desire of France's pre-revolutionary bourgeoisie to see themselves on stage. Voltaire and Diderot gave this audience tragedies, sentimental melodramas, and domestic comedies. An engraving by Jean Michel Moreau of Voltaire's 1732 Zaire is shown at lower left; a sketch of Diderot's 1757 The Illegitimate Son appears at upper left. Composer Jacques Offenbach amused later Parisian audiences with his spirited operettas (above). In sharp contrast were the horror shows at the Grand Guignol, as advertised in the poster below.

who saw theater as something more significant than a plaything of the ruling class were preparing a new theater aesthetic. They were somewhat like the romantics in their disapproval of the conservative establishment, but they broke with the earlier movement in coupling their disapproval with a clarion call for complete literalism and for a scientific confrontation with social facts. Led by the novelist Émile Zola, they espoused nothing less than "a theater of life." Zola, whose manifesto, *Naturalism in the Theater*, launched the new aesthetic in 1878 and provided it with a substantial terminology, quarreled not only with the official bourgeois theater but with the bourgeoisie itself. In his opinion both had chosen to remain ignorant of social reality, preferring to create a make-believe world in which social inequities did not exist.

Moreover, Zola objected vociferously to the picture of life portrayed on the stage of the Comédie Française. The empty, declamatory style of the acting then in vogue struck the novelist-playwright as false and evasive; he longed to create for the theatergoing public the same world he had created in his novels, a world of unadorned truth that submitted to clear, analytical, unemotional observation. In the preface to *Thérèse Raquin*, a play that Zola fashioned from his novel of the same name in 1873, the author insisted that the same intense, dispassionate realism so evident in his sociological novels should be presented in plays. He repeatedly employed the term "scientific" when giving instructions as to how the new aesthetic of realism should be applied in theater, and he was the first to stipulate that art should be an object of scientific investigation and knowledge rather than romantic or conservative reverence—an opinion that Marxist critics were later to claim as the starting point of the New Criticism. Further, Zola pitted himself against the literary language of official theater. He believed that the speech of the stage should be as down to earth and factual as "a police report or a court deposition." Indeed, Zola's choice of analogies, drawn mainly from science and law, reveals the extent to which he saw theater as an instrument of social justice, enlisting its full resources to make people conscious of social problems.

After first weathering a number of bouts with official censors, Zola's "slice of life" aesthetic caught on, revolutionizing acting and stage technology everywhere. In Paris, for example, André Antoine, spurred by Victor Hugo's concept of a free theater, was soon to change the course of theatrical history. Antoine, an avid theatergoer, was also an amateur actor who often served as an extra in the sumptuous productions of the Comédie Française. One evening after work he was invited by a friend to visit a group of amateur actors who put on boulevard plays to amuse themselves, their friends, and their families. Antoine willingly joined the group, which was directed by a retired army officer. The Circle, as it was called, rehearsed and performed in a small theater off a back alleyway.

From the first rehearsals, Antoine set about to convince the director that the actors should substitute a group of contemporary one acts—among them Zola's *Jacques Damour*—for their usual play by Eugène Scribe. The director disagreed, but Antoine was persistent. In the end he took over the direction of the group himself, immediately rechristening it the Théátre Libre in honor of Hugo. Antoine even succeeded in getting a critic from *Figaro*, France's leading literary newspaper, to attend the dress rehearsal of the first production, which took place on the evening of March 30, 1887. From the outset, it was obvious that something serious and worthwhile was happening in the tiny theater passageway of the Elysée des Beaux Arts—and when the next production opened two months later, all the critics were there for opening night.

Antoine, who held strong opinions on the necessity of theater reform, set out his views in *The Free Theater*, a red-covered publication that he both wrote and edited. The third, and in many ways the most critical, issue of *The Free Theater* contained the aesthetic princi-

ples of the theater of realism. As for the theater itself, here Antoine proposed a simple rectangular structure with bleacherlike risers for the audience. These seats, he declared, were to be arranged in such a way that every spectator sat parallel to the stage, insuring perfect sightlines and excellent acoustics. In this same vein he also wished to abolish the raked stage and to install lighting equipment that would produce more realistic illumination.

Antoine was, in time, to insist upon comfortable seats for the spectators, precautions against fire, and reform in ticket pricing, but it was his ideas on directing and acting that wrought the greatest changes in theater practice throughout the world. His rule of thumb was "Identify the milieu!"—by which he meant not only the physical but also the social and psychological environment of the play. Antoine believed, as did Zola and the naturalists, that all the indications for the actors' movements and speech were determined by environment, and he therefore launched his attack on the official theater practice of his day by providing the directives for a completely verisimile aesthetic.

From his unpretentious beginnings as an amateur actor, Antoine was eventually to rise to international eminence. The French government, acknowledging his importance, put the actor-director in charge of the Odéon, one of the state-subsidized theaters in Paris, in 1906. The Odéon thus became a showcase for Antoine's radical aesthetic, which was immediately accepted throughout Europe. Following his guidelines, theater companies were organized in London, Copenhagen, and Berlin. In Russia the Moscow Art Theater, which was to play such an important part in the development of naturalistic techniques in acting and theater production, was set up in accordance with the principles Antoine had established.

While Zola and Antoine were instigating their reforms in theater aesthetics and technology, the Norwegian playwright Henrik Ibsen was approaching the height of his career. After an initial struggle for recognition, Ibsen came to national notice in 1864 with a verse play, *Love's Comedy*, that won him a travel grant to Rome. There, a year later, he wrote his great poetic drama, *Brand*, which brought him international recognition. With recognition came a government pension that allowed him to write without financial worries, a godsend for which Ibsen was to remain grateful for the rest of his life. While still in Italy he wrote *Peer Gynt*, after which he abandoned verse as a dramatic form, adopting a more realistic style in which he addressed himself to the problems of contemporary, small-town society. Between 1877 and 1882 he wrote *The Pillars of Society*, *A Doll's House*, *Ghosts*, and *An Enemy of the People*, every one a marvel of dramatic skill and compelling realism.

During the years between 1884 and his death in 1906, Ibsen continued to write with the same mastery of the realistic style, but his persistent use of symbolism gave the plays he wrote the suggestion of a deeper set of considerations than the purely societal ones of the four earlier works. *The Wild Duck, Rosmersholm, The Lady from the Sea, Hedda Gabler, The Master Builder, Little Eyolf,* and *John Gabriel Borkman* are all dominated by symbols which, in spite of the familiarity of the characters and their environment, lend a note of deterministic fatalism to the action. In *When We Dead Awaken*, the last of his plays, Ibsen returns to the poetic form, although not to verse. This final play, completed in 1899, is about the last days of a financially successful but artistically bankrupt sculptor. Set in the never-never land of a sanitorium high in the snowy mountains, it is a beautiful, troubling elegy to Ibsen's accomplishments.

No nineteenth-century playwright was to have a greater impact upon contemporary theater, especially in England and America, than Ibsen. His technically triumphant plays, with their tightly fashioned dialogue and economic structure, became, collectively, a model of excellence for decades of young playwrights—and his deeply involving characters became the splendid vehicles for brilliant acting careers.

While Ibsen, already in his sixties and world famous, was writing his last plays, a young Russian named Anton Pavolovich Chekhov was drafting the first of the full-length, gently mordant comedies that would establish him as a writer of the caliber if not the productivity of the older playwright. A doctor by profession, Chekhov never considered his writing more than a hobby to be pursued in his spare time. However, both his short stories and dramatic works, although few in number, reveal phenomenal powers of psychological and social observation, subtle expression, and a sense of humor "sharp as horseradish."

Chekhov was passionately fond of the theater, and he began to write one-act playlets when he was still in his twenties. *The Bear, The Proposal*, and *The Marriage*, short plays in which he presented pretentious Russian provincials of his day in Gogol-like caricature, were all written between 1888 and 1890. They announce the subject matter of the full-length plays but have none of the sharpness of focus and subtle interplay of insight of the short stories or longer dramatic works. As a matter of fact, none of Chekhov's first full-length plays—not *Ivanov* in 1887; nor *The Wood Demon*, his early version of *Uncle Vanya*, writ-

It was André Antoine who introduced the Norwegian playwright Henrik Ibsen to Paris, although not until his plays had already been produced with success elsewhere in Europe. Opposite is a poster advertising a German performance of Ibsen's The Woman of the Sea; *the photograph above was taken during the first performance of* The Ghosts. *The Russian playwright Anton Chekhov never quite agreed with those who interpreted his insightful plays as pessimistic rather than optimistic. Nevertheless,* The Cherry Orchard *was presented in Moscow in 1904 (left, below) as a tragedy.*

129

ten in 1889; nor *The Seagull*, which was produced at the Alexandrinsky Theater in St. Petersburg—was successful.

Following the unfavorable reception of *The Seagull*, Chekhov began to question the advisability of showing his personal view of society to a public not yet ready for so intimate an exposé of middle-class futility. The playwright's wife, Olga, an actress associated with the new Moscow Art Theater, felt differently, however, and she enlisted Vladimir Nemirovich-Danchenko and Constantin Stanislavsky, the cofounders of the new theater, to persuade Chekhov that his plays, with their psychological and social insights, were just the sort of vehicles the new company was seeking. They argued that *The Seagull* should be given a new production at the Moscow Art Theater. Chekhov ultimately consented, and in 1898 the play was successfully restaged. Thus began one of the most famous and hotly disputed collaborations in theater history, one that involved Chekhov, his actress wife, Nemirovich-Danchenko, and Stanislavsky in the beginnings of an aesthetic of psychological realism that would dominate theater in Russia and the United States for half a century and ultimately influence every national theater in Western Europe.

Chekhov disagreed entirely with Stanislavsky's tragic interpretation of his plays. The playwright insisted that his characters were more comic than tragic in their frustrations, and he firmly believed that Russia would, one day, escape from the malaise he pictured. Stanislavsky favored a more romantic and sentimental reading of Chekhov's text, one that stressed the pathetic side of the trapped provincials and played down the element of hope. In spite of their differences of opinion, Chekhov continued to entrust his plays to Stanislavsky: first the new version of *The Wood Demon*, now called *Uncle Vanya*, in 1899; then, two years later, *The Three Sisters*; and finally in 1904, the year of his death, *The Cherry Orchard*. In each of these masterpieces Chekhov's wife played a principal role.

Both Ibsen and Chekhov presented a new world of determined, unheroic individualists trapped in a society that thwarted individualism and starved creativity; playwrights in other countries were soon treating the same subject in slightly different ways. In more than forty theater pieces, both short and long, the Swedish playwright August Strindberg created a much more brutal, violent, and agonized picture of the struggle between individuals and classes than had either Ibsen or Chekhov. His dark, lacerating plays, peopled with obsessed characters, herald the epoch of Freudianism. Like Ibsen, Strindberg began his career with poetic plays drawn from folk sources and national history, but with *The Father*, in 1887, he took up the subject that is central to most of his mature works: the inherent human capacity for evil. Although Strindberg sometimes turned to the world of dreams and fragmented reality for inspiration, his best-known plays treat obsessed individuals such as the eponymous protagonist of *Miss Julie*, a play that not only pits man against woman but servant against master.

Each of these playwrights inherited from the romantics a deep interest in the individual and his struggle with the demands of a society he had not chosen. Each, to a differing degree, presented a picture of

The scenography, advanced stage technology, and revolutionary costuming that Wagner envisioned were by no means perfectly realized through the facilities at Bayreuth when the festival was inaugurated in 1876. Indeed, the poetically powerful images of the Rhine maidens swimming in the watery depths, the ride of the Valkyries on their winged steeds, the entrance of the gods into Valhalla, and the magic fire in Wagner's titanic Ring Cycle were sometimes executed with almost comical naïveté at Bayreuth during Wagner's lifetime. Never-

theless, Wagner's ideas were later carried out with astonishing artistry under the direction of his heirs, and the Bayreuth festivals became synonymous with a distinctive expertise and excellence both in musical performances and stage technology.

The lighting effects that Wagner had suggested in his master plan for the Festspielhaus were finally realized by a Swiss technician, Adolphe Appia, sixteen years after Wagner's death. Appia's critical manifesto, *Music and Staging*, released in 1899, proposed both theoretical and practical extensions of Wagner's ideas on stage technology. The Swiss iconoclast, who viewed all dramatic productions as volume and movement in space, declared war on the painted trompe l'oeil scenery of the period. Convinced that stage lighting and painted scenery were incompatible, he sought to substitute multidimensional playing spaces at various levels and depths in relation to the spectator. Appia postulated that the actor, a three-dimensional being, was the center of all staging and could be best served by placing him in an environment made up of three-dimensional forms.

It was also Appia's contention that stage lighting, general and diffuse at the time, should be broken up into plots and modulated in color and intensity to accentuate and articulate the differences between spaces in the playing areas. He even formulated a set of axioms by which musical playing–time could be literally translated into space equivalents on the stage. Music, he claimed, determined the exact dimensions of any performing area and its placement in relation to the rest of the stage space. The invention of electric light and high intensity lamps made Appia's theories on stage lighting perfectly feasible, but the theater public's interest in naturalism, with its simple lighting demands, prevented his ideas from being widely accepted for almost two additional decades.

Ten years before Wagner presented his first season at the Bayreuth Festspielhaus, George II, Duke of Saxe-Meiningen, created an acting company at his court that was to achieve international fame and serve as a model for future arts theaters. The duke was neither a poet, a revolutionary, nor a theoretician, but his devotion to theater was absolute, and under his aegis the weak, provincial court theater of Saxe-Meiningen was transformed into an impeccable ensemble. The very existence of such a company, although its qualities were modest in comparison to Wagner's grandiose visions, was living proof that the Arts Theater Movement's aspirations could be realized. There were no outstanding

actors in the duke's company, only devoted ones. As a result, training and discipline were excellent, and many of the actors and technicians who worked for the duke became individually famous after 1890, when the company ceased touring.

It is not clear how the duke, an officer in the royal guard until his accession to the dukedom in 1866, had learned what he knew about directing actors, designing and mounting productions, and adapting texts, but he seemed to be expert in all of these areas. With the help of his actress-wife and an actor named Ludwig Chromegk, the duke not only built an excellent repertory group but also made it financially profitable. In the course of eighty tours that the company made between 1874 and 1890, the Meiningers won international acclaim in cities as distant as Brussels, London, and Odessa.

Both André Antoine and Stanislavsky saw performances of the Meininger troupe, and both were deeply impressed with the group's ensemble work. The duke himself chose and adapted the plays, principally from Shakespeare, Schiller, and Molière, designed the sets and costumes, and directed the productions. From the very first he rehearsed the actors on the actual set, and in costume, until they attained something of the precision of an expert military drill team. He also took great pains to research the periods of the plays he chose, producing costumes, settings, and properties that were historically correct in every detail. His special skill lay in maneuvering the actors in crowd scenes, a knack he apparently learned from the English actor-manager

Charles Kean, whom he had observed in rehearsals during frequent visits to London in his youth.

The most remarkable attributes of the Meininger Company were its consistent devotion to every detail of dramatic art and its disciplined execution of the duke's artistic direction. The perfect coordination of the elements of each production and the quietly powerful effect of the troupe's ensemble playing were in striking contrast to the badly coordinated productions and the virtuoso playing so common in the late nineteenth century. The Meininger Company thus became the model for artistic reform in theater, a paradigm of the perfect arts theater.

The most influential proponent of the Arts Theater Movement was the English designer, producer, and theorist Edward Gordon Craig. Craig, who was born in 1872, lived until 1966, and although he retired from active participation in theater production at the end of the 1920's, he continued to exert a powerful influence over the Arts Theater Movement from his retreat in the south of France. Through his book, *The Art of the Theatre*, and his magazine, *The Mask*, which he published at irregular intervals for twenty years, Craig was to affect the nature of modern theater production everywhere.

Edward Gordon Craig was the son of the famous English actress Ellen Terry, and following a tradition of the Terry family he began to act in plays in London as a very young child. From his earliest years he was surrounded by actors, directors, designers, technicians, and writers, and he spent his twenties acting at the London Lyceum under the direction of Henry Irving. While at the Lyceum, Craig had occasion to observe the work of England's leading designer, Rawes Craven, who taught him the principles of electric lighting, a recent invention that was to revolutionize staging.

At thirty Craig abandoned a promising acting career to devote himself entirely to designing, directing, writing, and teaching. He settled for a short time in Florence, where, in 1906, he collaborated for the first time with Adolphe Appia. Together they designed a production of Ibsen's *Rosmersholm* for Eleonora Duse, Italy's première actress. The young Englishman's association with Appia, whose ideas on theater production Craig found most congenial, was to last until Appia's death in 1928. Appia, the senior member of the partnership by a full decade, was shy, unobtrusive, quiet; Craig, on the other hand, was outrageously handsome, flamboyant, and aggressively articulate. Their collaboration was an immensely successful one nonetheless, and through Craig's well-illustrated magazine they were to dictate the guidelines for the future development of the Arts Theater Movement.

Indeed, there was scarcely an aspect of theater aesthetics and tech-

The theater was a small world for designer Edward Gordon Craig. The noted English actress Ellen Terry was his mother, and consequently he grew up on stage, playing such roles as that of Cromwell (left, below) in Henry VIII. He also designed productions for the internationally known Italian actress Eleonora Duse, shown opposite as the tragic heroine of Shakespeare's Antony and Cleopatra; and he collaborated with the dynamic Isadora Duncan, depicted in the watercolor at right, on the basics of stage movement.

JOSÉ-CLARÁ

nology that Craig did not discuss in *The Mask*. He used the magazine as a forum to advance his ideas on acting and the training of actors. Collaborating with the Swiss composer and eurhythmics expert Emile Jaques-Dalcroze and the legendary American dancer Isadora Duncan, he developed the neglected area of stage movement. Craig also traveled widely, especially in France and Germany, where he sparked important theater reforms. He was even called to Russia to design the Moscow Art Theater's 1912 production of *Hamlet*—despite the fact that he and Stanislavsky were in disagreement on many aspects of theater production. Craig was especially opposed to the notion of intense psychological identification between the actor and his role—the hallmark of the Stanislavsky method—demanding instead a superbly trained actor who was capable of carrying out selflessly every desire of the director.

By the time of Appia's death in 1928 he and Craig had become the accepted prophets of the theater's future in Europe and America. Their many books and articles—coupled with published portfolios of renderings of their theories and projects—were eagerly received everywhere, and their advice was universally sought and almost universally heeded. Jacques Copeau, the father of modern French theater, openly admitted his debt to Craig and Appia when, in 1913, he set up the actors' training program at the Vieux-Colombier, a center of instruction and performance in Paris where such leaders of theater reform as Louis Jouvet, Charles Dullin, Etienne Decroux, the Fratellini brothers, and Copeau's nephew, Michel St. Denis, were trained. England's Old Vic, founded in 1914 by Lilian Baylis, was also to feel the informative force of Appia and Craig—largely through the efforts of Michel St. Denis, who created its training program.

In the twenties and early thirties, New York was likewise a center of theatrical interest and activity. The tenets of Appia and Craig were widely discussed, and they served as touchstones for such noted designers as Robert Edmond Jones and Norman Bel Geddes. Copeau's company spent two years in New York, and Max Reinhardt, the director of

LE VIEUX-COLOMBIER IN ENGLAND

MARCH 1914

(THE TIMES)

...It is not yet six months since the THEATRE DU VIEUX COLOMBIER was started, and it is only four since a correspondent of THE TIMES, in an article on "THE FRENCH REPERTORY MOVEMENT" declared that "its inauguration may fairly be regarded as the most significant event in the history of the modern French drama since the foundation of the

41

The influence of the symbolists Appia and Craig was seen in Paris in 1913 when Jacques Copeau established his antirealist Théâtre du Vieux-Colombier, mentioned in the English newspaper clipping above. The photograph at left, a scene from The Brothers Karamazov, *shows Copeau seated (left) at a table. He stands at right, above, dressed as Scapin for a 1920 production of Molière's* Les fourberies de Scapin. *Symbolist scenery appears at far right in Emil Orlik's sketch of Austrian director Max Reinhardt during a rehearsal.*

the Deutsches Theater and the foremost exponent of Craig's teaching concerning the master director, also spent much time in America. However, it was the visit of the Moscow Art Theater, more than the teachings of Craig and Appia, that impressed American actors and directors in the 1920's. The ensemble's realistic acting technique, embodying the essence of Stanislavsky's teachings, struck an especially congenial tone. In fact, Stanislavsky's introspective approach to acting so fascinated the members of the Group Theater in New York that they adopted it as the basis for their own "method," which was to continue to evolve throughout the thirties. Indeed, in the space of a few years, this method was to become the prevailing American acting style.

It would be inappropriate to close a chapter on the Arts Theater Movement without mentioning the Ballet Russe. In its use of painted

scenery and elaborately designed costumes, the ballet was in diametric opposition to the teachings of Appia and Craig. Nevertheless, its ability to attract the finest designers, painters, technicians, composers, choreographers, and performers—all under the strict artistic direction of Sergei Diaghilev—made that great innovative ensemble a fine working example of the Arts Theater Movement, one that was to have a deep and lasting effect upon theater training, planning, technology, artistic coordination, and management well into the twentieth century.

William Saroyan, and Clifford Odets were among the writers whose early plays were produced by the Group Theater.

Eugene O'Neill, who had already won a Pulitzer Prize in 1920 for *Beyond the Horizon*, had evinced some interest in writing distinctly American plays—and *Desire Under the Elms* and *Ah, Wilderness!* are unquestionably works with special flavor and authenticity. Yet O'Neill was obsessed with researching certain European genres, especially the expressionistic plays of Scandinavia and Germany, and both *The Hairy Ape* and *The Great God Brown* are byproducts of that predilection.

O'Neill's deepest interest lay in the mythic tragedies of ancient Greece, however. His trilogy, *Mourning Becomes Electra*, finished in 1931, is an Americanization of the *Oresteia* in which O'Neill substitutes New England for Aeschylus' Mycenae, and the American Civil War for the Trojan War. In 1936, the same year that he was awarded the Nobel Prize for Literature, the ailing playwright retired. He continued to write, but he systematically denied performance rights to his new plays. In retirement, O'Neill's long years of experimentation with classic forms, archetypes, ancient mythic elements, and his life experience coalesced perfectly in his greatest play, *Long Day's Journey Into Night*. Ironically, that work was not produced until 1956, three years after O'Neill's death.

The mid-twentieth century marked the apogee of American drama. Three stage classics of the period were Arthur Miller's Death of a Salesman, *starring Lee J. Cobb and Mildred Dunnock (above); Eugene O'Neill's* Long Day's Journey Into Night, *with Jason Robards, Fredric March, and Florence Eldridge (below); and Tennessee Williams'* A Streetcar Named Desire, *with Marlon Brando and Jessica Tandy (opposite).*

Eugene O'Neill's masterful, if uneven, use of the mythic elements of drama distinguish him from other great American playwrights of the twentieth century. Tennessee Williams, in such plays as *The Glass Menagerie* and *A Streetcar Named Desire*, clearly surpasses O'Neill in compassion, warmth, and lyricism. And Arthur Miller's *Death of a Salesman* succeeds more surely in capturing a recognizable American archetype, Willy Loman. Yet the scope of O'Neill's vision is titanic and mythic, while both Williams' and Miller's remain tightly focused.

During the 1920's the Broadway musical, now widely thought to be the United States' unique contribution to the universal list of theater genres, came into being. Its forebears were certainly the Viennese operettas of Franz Lehar and Oscar Straus. Yet the musical differs from them in that it utilizes a credible plot, music and lyrics of equal importance, strong chorus and ensemble work, and expert choreography. Unlike the earlier operettas and musical comedies in which the company was clearly divided into musicians, dancers, and actors, the Broadway musical requires a cast in which every member can sing, dance, and act with skill and energy. These demands have for two decades dictated the training policies of most of the leading theater schools in the United States.

In the 1920's Jerome Kern, George Gershwin, and Vincent Youmans defined the Broadway musical through such productions as *Showboat*, *Lady Be Good*, and *Hit the Deck*, but the genre really came of age with Richard Rodgers and Oscar Hammerstein's *Oklahoma!* in 1943. In the hands of Cole Porter, Irving Berlin, Leonard Bernstein, Stephen Sondheim, and many others it has developed into an admirable theater form, the undisputed favorite of American theatergoers.

In advocating the Arts Theater Movement, Wagner and Craig had hoped to wrench theater free from unimaginative, commercial manag-

ers and create a hegemony for "priests of art." Neither Wagner nor Craig had foreseen the enormous chasm that was soon to open between art and society in general—although Craig, during his long lifetime, was to see that process effected. Conventional form simply disintegrated, and the ensuing fragmentation was felt in every quarter: literature, painting, sculpture, music, dance, and of course theater.

As the cement of convention lost its binding force, the elements of communication became more identifiable as individual entities than they had ever been in the memory of man. In literature the multiplicity of meanings inherent in words was explored by such artists as Gertrude Stein and James Joyce, who cut language loose from traditional grammar and syntax. In painting, the dimensional syntax of conventional drawing was discarded by Picasso and Braque, who were among the founders of Cubism. Sculptors, composers, architects, and choreographers followed suit, reexamining and rediscovering the basic communicative elements of their art. Theater, already under the close scrutiny inspired by general discontent on the part of serious artists everywhere, naturally succumbed to this upheaval.

The most striking and perhaps the most trenchant observer of this general disintegration and its specific application was Antonin Artaud. In 1910, at the age of five, Artaud almost succumbed to meningitis, and the disease left him with permanent brain damage that grew progressively worse. The Frenchman's extraordinary powers of observation allowed him to study the disintegration of his own mind with the objectivity of a scientist and the subjectivity of a poet.

As he struggled to give exact expression to the steps of his psychic deterioration and the consequent failure of his habitual thought processes, Artaud saw himself as a microcosm of the general process of disintegration in communication between the artist and society. He began

The musical, America's glossy packaging of the Viennese operetta, emerged as a major theatrical genre in 1943 with Richard Rodgers and Oscar Hammerstein's Oklahoma! *Above, members of the original cast surround the celebrated "surrey with the fringe on top." At the other end of the theatrical spectrum stood men like Jean-Louis Barrault, a reformer who was trying to reach a more basic level of theatrical communication. The mime Barrault is shown at right as Baptiste in a wordless production of William Faulkner's* As I Lay Dying.

to feel that there was a surer level of communication than words—a suspicion confirmed in 1931 when he witnessed a production of the Balinese theater at the Colonial Exhibition in Paris. In watching this wordless performance with its moving language of gesture, sound, and dramatic tension, Artaud was convinced that he had discovered the process by which Western theater could bypass the ruined language of words and with gesture, cries, and ritual reach a defenseless area of direct communication. Artaud eventually elaborated his plans for a "theater of cruelty" in a series of essays, and in 1935 he applied some of those theories in a Parisian production of *The Cover*, which ran for only seventeen performances. Parisian audiences detested it, and the critics were abusive.

Artaud never saw his theater of cruelty principles taken seriously during his lifetime, although he felt that the Marx Brothers had created something near to it in *Animal Crackers* and *Monkey Business*. He also felt that Jean-Louis Barrault's mime based on Faulkner's *As I Lay Dying* had achieved through gesture the kind of direct, primitive communication he had hoped to produce in his theater of cruelty. Not until 1966, twenty years after his death, were Artaud's neglected ideas to receive the major consideration they merited. And even then the exposure was to come not in Artaud's own country but in England, where a series of experimental performances was undertaken by the Royal Shakespeare Company under the direction of Peter Brook.

Artaud, and before him Appia and Craig, had tried to reform theater through radical reevaluations of its special language and technology. None of the three ever thought of theater as anything other than an exacting, revered art. The opposite view was held by the German playwrights Erwin Piscator and Bertolt Brecht, who initiated their theater reforms along Marxist lines. In order to bring theater to the proletariat they insisted that reverence for art sprang from bourgeois sources and that, in accordance with Marx's teachings, art was properly an object of knowledge, not reverence. To this end they set out to destroy the emotional hold of Wagner's theater. Through technological means Wagner had created an overpowering, emotional atmosphere sustained by lowered house lights, hidden musicians, and sentimental music, all in the service of an artistic and ethnic myth. They demanded that the houselights never be covered, that the audience be allowed to smoke, that all the technical elements be in plain view. Since they maintained that theater should teach, they insisted that an atmosphere of challenging doubt ought to be maintained.

Piscator saw theater as an instrument of class struggle, a truly propagandistic pursuit. To break the illusion of traditional productions, he divided his presentations into episodes, often rewriting the text in the process. A man of prodigious energy and great resourcefulness, Piscator was constantly on the move—and constantly exploring new technical possibilities. During World War II he taught in New York, but in 1951 he returned to Germany, where he continued to direct interesting and provocative productions until his death in 1966.

Bertolt Brecht was not only an excellent poet and playwright, he was also a superb director and manager who profoundly influenced the style of modern theater productions. It is hardly surprising then that Brecht's work, although ideologically allied to that of Piscator, frequently exceeded the merely ideological. An avowed opponent of Wagnerian theater, Brecht not only espoused Piscator's epic theater but developed it—in such major plays as *Mother Courage and Her Children, The Caucasian Chalk Circle, Galileo Galilei,* and *The Good Woman of Setzuan*—into a universally recognized genre.

Brecht first achieved fame with a rewriting of John Gay's *The Beggar's Opera,* from which, with the collaboration of Kurt Weill, he fashioned the modern masterpiece *The Threepenny Opera.* It was the beginning of a long and successful partnership. Brecht fled Nazi Germany but returned after World War II to create and direct the Berliner Ensemble in East Berlin. His directing feats are legendary, and thanks to his mania for keeping notes and making photographic records of his productions, his methods are widely known and imitated.

Neither Artaud's ideas nor those of Piscator and Brecht have checked the process by which theater, as an art form, has grown increasingly personal and individual in both its language and vision. This process of disintegration and fragmentation, which began to concern many serious artists in every field of creative activity before World War I, continued after World War II with greater and more widespread vigor. In this atmosphere Artaud, who had received little serious attention outside France during his lifetime, achieved, during the 1960's, the status of a prophet-martyr. His violently worded theater of cruelty manifestos, which appealed to the growing spirit of revolt, became the professed articles of faith for many experimental theater groups, the

most typical of which was the Living Theater. Under the direction of Julian Beck and his wife, Judith Malina, this group of performers became a living rebuke to conventional economics, culture, and politics. During the height of the student unrest of the 1960's, the Living Theater, by then an enormous traveling commune, took an active part in the dramatization of student manifestos, performing throughout West Germany and France.

As has already been noted, the English director Peter Brook spent several years researching Artaud's theater of cruelty with members of the Royal Shakespeare Company, deriving from his experiments the much–discussed production of *The Persecution and Assassination of Marat as Performed by the Inmates of the Asylum of Charenton under the Direction of the Marquis de Sade* in 1964. Among those who

In Brecht's Mother Courage and Her Children *(opposite), the protagonist does little more than survive, suggesting that simply staying alive amidst chaos and assault is itself a heroic task. So too theater survives, moving on to new forms and revitalizing old ones. These include the masked performances of the Bread and Puppet Theater (right) as well as the freeform productions of the Living Theater (overleaf).*

assisted Brook in the experiments were Jerzy Grotowski, director of the Polish Laboratory Theater, and Joseph Chaikin, director of the New York Open Theater. Each of these young directors has a record of a decade of patient experimentation with the fundamentals of theater and the education of the actor. Along with Grotowski's disciple Eugenio Barta in Denmark, they have become major formative forces in contemporary experimental theater.

Other theater groups, among them Luis Valdez' Teatro Campesino in California's San Joaquin Valley and Peter Schumann's Bread and Puppet Theater in New York, have accepted the dictates of Piscator and Brecht, creating a theater of instruction—and playing, for the most part, out-of-doors. Following the example of these two lively companies, many young street ensembles now perform in parks, playgrounds, and parking lots—giving the lie to the notion, uttered over a century ago, that theater is dead.

Judging from appearances alone, one might conclude that with the passing of sumptuous Renaissance theater and the elaborate conventions of that theater's protocol, something has indeed died—but forms, as Plato reminded us long ago, are only forms; they are not the essence. The essence of theater is the imitation of life, whatever the circumstances of life at any given moment happen to be. And one thing is certain: as long as man survives, theater and the imitative act, the essential function of all language, will continue—choosing, as circumstances dictate, that form which most closely suits its immediate purpose.

MEMOIRS OF
THEATRICAL LIVES

Moss Hart was a lucky creature of the theater. While still a young man, he secured George S. Kaufman as coauthor and director for a play he had drafted, Once in a Lifetime. *Many years later, Hart recounted the anxieties and pleasures that attended the first of his many Broadway successes.*

The golden rule for the last three days before an opening is that a company must be kept together as constantly as possible, even if some of the rehearsals that are called are purely trumped-up ones and fool nobody, including the company itself. If it is impossible to rehearse on the stage because the scenery is not yet set up, or the scenic designer is still lighting it as he always interminably is, then the rehearsal is held in the lounge of the theatre or in a rehearsal hall. Almost nothing is accomplished, for the actors walk through these rehearsals in a state approximating somnambulism, but the rule and the theory behind it is a sound one. Left to their own devices, a company might conceivably gain the impression that the world had not stopped in its tracks for these three days and that all life did not hang in the balance of those two and a half hours three nights hence. Moreover, misery does indeed love company, and there is nothing so soothing, not to say downright invigorating, as the shared misery of people in the same boat. Tempers may flare and patience reach the vanishing point, but temper or even the drudgery of walking through the play in an empty rehearsal hall can be a safety valve for taut nerves, can prevent the panic that can rise in a company left to wander too loosely in these last days.

If I had been inclined to doubt the rightness of this procedure, all of my reservations would have vanished by the afternoon of the day following my return from Philadelphia. I had passed the morning easily enough in telephoning, but by mid-afternoon I could scarcely stay in my skin. Though I knew no rehearsal was scheduled until the next morning at eleven, I could not remain away from the theatre. I had no idea why I felt it imperative to be there, but I took the subway into town, and at the first glimpse of the scenery piled up on the street outside the Music Box as I turned the corner of 45th Street I felt immediately better. I moved toward it with a lift of the heart and hurried through the stage door as though I were leaving enemy territory for the safety of the U. S. Marines. There are few things duller to watch than scenery being set up on a stage, but that afternoon I found this dull business comforting beyond measure. I watched every bit of it with pleasure and even fascination. I sat or walked up and down in the aisles of the empty theatre hour after hour, or wandered backstage and swilled coffee with the stagehands, and knew that this peace I felt would last only as long as I remained here. . . .

The company, when they assembled for rehearsal the next morning, greeted each other with the hungry affection of exiles returning to their native land. They had evidently spent a completely miserable day with their husbands, their wives, their cats or their tropical fish, and were happy to be back among their own kind, amidst people who were using the only language they cared to hear spoken at this particular moment. . . .

On the day before a New York opening, a company moves within a solar system of its own. It is a planet in outer space, detached from the moon and stars, and its orbit is the stairway from the dressing rooms to the stage. Each actor sits at his make-up table, staring into the brilliantly lit mirror at his own image, making the proscribed movements that will detach him still further from the world of reality and allow him to achieve the anonymity of complete disguise. The more he becomes at one with the part he is to play, the less of himself that peeps through it, the further he sinks into the atmosphere of make-believe and unreality, the safer he feels. He is seeking a judgment from the real world, not of himself but of the hidden image he carries within him that is both his goal and his refuge. . . .

It was just as well that I had reconciled myself to a bad rehearsal, for the proceedings on the stage of the Music Box were more like a series of nervous explosions than anything else. Hats and dresses that had fit perfectly well in Philadelphia seemed to have come back from the cleaners a size too small. Entrances were missed or exits bungled, and doors that had opened with ease and props that handled without difficulty before, now presented mysterious problems each time one was open or picked up. Mr. Kaufman rode out the storm like a pilot searching out the eye of a hurricane—unruffled, detached and ready to report back to the weather bureau that the storm was not a dangerous one. But by the end of the afternoon rehearsal I was in no such state of calm. If the final run-through tonight emerged looking anything like this one, I doubted my capacity to sit through it, or perhaps even to live through it. . . .

There is no need to try to understand the eternal perverseness of the theatre, or to attempt to explain why an afternoon rehearsal can be a shambles and an evening rehearsal on the same day be orderly, smooth and perfect in every detail. Like a good deal of the theatre's disorderliness, it defies explanation. It is simpler to say that the evening run-through of *Once in a Lifetime* was flawless. Every mistake of the afternoon had corrected itself; every error in light cues, every blunder in props, every imperfection in costume had vanished. The rehearsal was faultless except in one particular: the acting was completely hollow. Its emptiness may have been due to the difficulty of playing comedy in an empty theatre, for a preview audience the night before an opening was the exception, not the rule, in those days. But granting this difficulty and making all allowances for it, it was hard not to be aware of the falsity of the playing. Not one performance carried conviction. Each actor seemed to lack fluidity, bounce or humor, and in consequence the play very soon took on the patina of its acting. By the time the final curtain fell, the play seemed to me to be as brittle and humorless as the performance. . . .

THE MUSIC BOX

ONCE IN A LIFETIME

Playbill for the original production of Once in a Lifetime

I walked toward *Once in a Lifetime* for the last time—that final walk every playwright takes toward his play, knowing that it is no longer his, that it belongs to the actors and the audience now, that a part of himself is to be judged by strangers and that he can only watch it as a stranger himself. The main consideration of his day, the keystone that has dictated his every waking moment, the cause that has enlisted his being for all these months, is at an end. He moves toward his destination with mixed emotions—it is the completion he has sought, but there is the ache of finality in it. He is at last a spectator—a spectator with the largest stake in the gamble of the evening, but a spectator nonetheless. . . .

Not until I heard Max Siegel's [the assistant producer] voice saying to the stage manager, "They're all in; take the house lights down," could I bring myself to move. I walked through the pass door into the theatre, and in the half-light I peeked through the curtain below the stage box to steal a quick look at the audience—that foolish and hopeful look a playwright sometimes takes in those last few minutes before the curtain rises. . . .

The curtain was rising, and Hugh O'Connell and the set were receiving their regulation round of applause. Jean Dixon made her entrance, the applause swelled, and as it died down she spoke the opening lines. I held my breath to wait for the first laugh, which always came on her second or third line. No sound, however, appeared to be issuing from her lips. One could see her lips moving, but that was all. No sound came forth. Hugh O'Connell spoke, but no sound came from his lips, either. They seemed to be two people talking to each other behind a glass wall.

The audience began to murmur and turn to each other in their seats. My heart skipped a beat and I looked wildly toward Mr. Kaufman. He stood frozen in his tracks, staring at the stage. Jean Dixon and Hugh O'connell were talking steadily on, unaware that they could not be heard, but aware that something was gravely wrong, for the murmur from the audience was loud enough for them to hear it now and I could see Jean Dixon's hand shake as she lit a cigarette. Still no sound came from the stage, and in the silence a man's voice from the balcony rang out loud and clear: "It's the fans—turn off the fans!"

The audience broke into relieved laughter and applause. I saw Mr. Kaufman make a dash for the pass door that led backstage, but before he was halfway down the aisle, the fans on either side of the proscenium began to slow down. In the opening-night excitement, the electrician had simply forgotten to turn off the fans—one of those simple little opening-night mistakes that lessen the life span of everyone concerned by five or ten years! The nightmare had lasted no more than a minute in all, but it is not one of the minutes I should choose to live over again. Invariably, when horrors of this kind occur, the audience behaves admirably and they did so now. They not only applauded that unknown hero in the balcony, but they rewarded Jean Dixon with a generous round of applause when she went back and started the scene all over again. She could not, of course, go off the stage and re-enter, but aware that not a word of the scene had been heard, she calmly took a puff or two of her cigarette, waited until the fans·had stopped, and began the scene anew.

From that moment onward, both play and audience took on something of the quality of fantasy—it was being played and received like a playwright's dream of a perfect opening night. The performance was brilliant and the audience matched it in their response. . . .

Moss HART
Act One, 1959

George S. Kaufman, the most successful playwright-director in Broadway history, always worked in collaboration with another author. The talents of Marc Connelly, Moss Hart, and Edna Ferber complemented Kaufman's own abilities and produced outstanding musicals and comedies. Howard Teichman, yet another of his collaborators, describes the sometimes comic circumstances that surrounded Kaufman's alliance with Edna Ferber.

In her first autobiography, *A Peculiar Treasure*, Miss Ferber conveyed her impression of Kaufman: "Ah, here comes the Duke now!" A duke at the very least is what Edna Ferber thought George Kaufman really was, although in conversation she said of him, "He was like a dry cracker. Brittle."

In many ways she was very much like Kaufman: middle-western birthplace, same German-Jewish background, same training as a newspaper reporter, same discipline toward work.

In other ways she was the direct opposite of Kaufman. She was small in physical stature, and a great believer in exercise. She had great personal courage, an overwhelming desire to travel, to seek new people, new places, new ideas. She did not have Kaufman's wit, but she did have the ability to write rich, deep love scenes.

Edna Ferber was already a well-known short-story writer (the Emma McChesney stories) and novelist (*Dawn O'Hara* and *So Big*). It was Beatrice [Kaufman's wife] who brought them together. Bea had bought a volume containing "Old Man Minick," one of Miss Ferber's better short stories, and had recommended it to George to read. He did. When he was convinced it could be made into a play, she urged him to write the author.

Miss Ferber and Mr. Kaufman met at the Kaufman apartment. Once they decided to collaborate on the play, they followed a new Kaufman theory: get away from the telephone, friends, family, everyone and everything, and concentrate on playwriting.

In a White Plains hotel, George and Edna sequestered themselves. At a concentrated but still astounding pace, they wrote *Minick* in three or four days. "Anything to escape from that awful hotel," Kaufman liked to say in later years.

Minick was a hit.

The Royal Family (1927), the next Kaufman-Ferber play, took time more in keeping with Kaufman's "ten minutes a day" line. Kaufman liked to tell people it took two years to write a play with Miss Ferber. "That is," Kaufman said, "because Edna works from nine A.M. to three-ten P.M., and I work from three P.M. to nine P.M., which gives us ten minutes a day in which to collaborate."

Having decided to do a play about a theatrical family—not similar enough to the Barrymores, whom they both knew quite well, but also different enough from the Barrymores to gain approval from their respective lawyers—Kaufman and Ferber spent eight entire months writing it.

Each morning, promptly at the stroke of eleven, George would arrive at Edna's apartment on Central Park West. As she was a lady and had the choice of sitting or standing, Edna chose the chair in front of the typewriter. This freed George to pace constantly, tie and untie his shoe laces, stretch out on the couches, indulge in small idiosyncrasies such as making faces at Edna, gossiping, twirling curtain cords, and the like.

"My God," he once complained to her, "everyone has telephoned this morning except Queen Mary!"

Lunch was served in the Ferber household at one-thirty: sandwiches and coffee, which George wasn't wild about, and pastry and chocolate candy, which he savored.

Work would stop when George felt it was time for him to appear at his bridge club. But even a six-hour day, month in and month out, was not time enough to lick *The Royal Family*. To do that, they had to fall back on the Kaufman theory: isolation.

Edna had chosen the hotel for *Minick*. George was given the choice for *The Royal Family*.

Brooklyn. The St. George Hotel. Adjoining rooms.

Edna never quite understood why he chose Brooklyn, but she went along. All she insisted on was that when they finished work for the night, George retire to his room to get enough rest for the next day's work.

And he did retire. Until he was certain Edna was alseep. Then he would quietly let himself out and take the subway into Manhattan, where he was having an affair with a very demanding young woman. Early in the morning, he would return to the St. George Hotel, catch a few hours' sleep, and be ready for work with Edna at eleven.

Although they finished the play, although it was a hit, although Edna said she'd rather work with George than anyone else, she never wanted to go back to Brooklyn. She said it didn't agree with George; he never looked rested those days.

Later in their collaboration Miss Ferber acquired a country house, and for a while they worked there. Frequently, however, an impatient buzzer would sound; Edna would excuse herself and leave the room. A few minutes later, she'd return, work would resume, and then the buzzer would sound again.

Infuriated by these interruptions, George demanded an explanation. "Well, here in the country, help is so hard to get that I don't ring for the servants," she said. "When they want something, they send for me."

"They're acting like actors, Edna," he bristled. "Pretty soon they'll want their names above the title of this play."

HOWARD TEICHMAN
George S. Kaufman: An Intimate Portrait, 1972

During the 1920's and 30's the Theatre Guild brought a high quality of serious drama and sophisticated comedy to Broadway. Although the Guild attracted many fine talents, none were more important to its success than Alfred Lunt and Lynn Fontanne. Lawrence Langner, one of the Guild's founders and a close observer of the Lunts' career, describes the qualities that made them such consummate actors.

THE PLAYBILL
FOR · THE · ALVIN · THEATRE

Alfred Lunt and Lynn Fontanne in The Taming of the Shrew

... Alfred Lunt and Lynn Fontanne had written a vivid page in the history of the American theatre. ... The couple brought such zest and vitality to their acting, and there was such interplay of point and counterpoint in their scenes together, that soon one began to think of them almost as one personality—named Lynn-and-Alfred—a personality capable of miraculously endowing every couple they portrayed with the qualities of beauty, charm, wit, gaiety and enormous interest in one another. "How can any other actors expect to play together as well as Alfred and Lynn?" complained an actress bitterly. "They rehearse in bed!" "Would you like to meet Alfred and Lynn backstage and congratulate them on their acting?" I asked George Bernard Shaw after he had seen and liked them in *Caprice*. "It's not acting," said Shaw. "It's performing!"

Alfred and Lynn have made only one motion picture, *The Guardsman*, so that posterity may at least take a look at them as they were when they played in this masterpiece of light comedy. But no picture can convey the sheer delight which the audiences of our time have enjoyed in watching their virtuoso acting, which can range, as occasions demand, from delicate sentiment to deep emotion and tragedy, from moods of gaiety and light laughter to the savage laughter of satire or irony. When the Lunts played a comedy scene together, you felt you were watching the iridescent darting of lights and color all over the stage—the gods of the theatre were good to the public when they brought them together, and they were good to the Theatre Guild when all three of us joined hands for the future.

Alfred and Lynn, both of them tall, slender and invariably well-turned out, always appear calm and cool at rehearsals of their plays. They work without sparing themselves, paying the minutest attention to the minutest details. If they are tired or worried over whether a scene is going properly or needs rewriting, it is Alfred who usually shows sign of nerves. No matter what Lynn may be feeling, she always keeps herself well in hand, and where Alfred might be emotional or temperamental, she can be counted on to calm him down ... If a play has an excellent part for Alfred, but not for Lynn, Alfred can be counted on to tell us that it is Lynn's turn to have the better part; and Lynn will be equally concerned for Alfred. This made it quite difficult to find plays for them, until Robert Sherwood learned the formula of making the parts substantially equal. "What is the secret of your success in the theatre?" someone once asked Sherwood. "I write plays for the Lunts," he replied.

Once the play has opened, Alfred and Lynn treat it in a manner which is rare in the theatre. No mother could take care of her babies more conscientiously than the Lunts take care of their plays. Each performance is for them of equal importance. "It's cheating the public to take their money and then let down," I have often heard Lynn remark. And they demand from their company the same attitude toward their work ... Fooling on stage, breaking up other actors, and other devices for relieving the tedium of consecutive performances, are taboo with the Lunts, who work ceaselessly to deepen their parts and to find better ways of playing them ... After playing *O Mistress Mine* for three years, during the last Saturday matinee Alfred said to young Dick Van Patten, playing the juvenile, "I have a new idea for this scene. I think it will improve it. We have one more chance to try it before we close the play!" ...

Lawrence Langner
The Magic Curtain, 1951

National tours of hit plays are an important part of theatrical tradition. As the company moves from city to city both the normal routines of everyday life and extraordinary personal events take second place to the job at hand. The following account of a tour of The Little Foxes, *starring Tallulah Bankhead, illustrates the high degree of professionalism such ventures demand.*

... Tallulah and Eugenia Rawls immediately started rehearsing for the national tour of *The Little Foxes*. The play was booked to travel some twenty-five thousand miles, zigzagging from coast to coast over an intricate cat's cradle of rail lines that have long since given up passenger service; in the course of the long journey, the company would be called on to play the astonishing total of eighty-seven consecutive one-night stands. The play opened in Princeton, on Saturday, September 14. Shortly before curtain-time, Tallulah received a message from Wash-

160

Tallulah Bankhead in The Little Foxes

ington: Speaker Will [Miss Bankhead's father] was dying and she must come at once. The house was sold out and people were beginning to take their seats; Tallulah decided to play. After the performance, she was driven to Princeton Junction, where it had been arranged for a Washington express train to stop for her. By the time she reached the hospital in Washington, Speaker Will was dead. A state funeral was held for him in the capitol on the following Monday, after which, with the help of a police escort, Tallulah was driven to Hershey in time for her performance. As so often happens in the presence of death, the lines of the play took on new meanings. At one point, Regina says to Alexandra, "Tell your Papa that I want him to come home again, that I love him very much," and at another, "You've had a bad shock today. I know that. And you loved Papa, but you must have expected this to come someday. You knew how sick he was." Tallulah spoke the lines without flinching.

The tour was as successful as it was strenuous. Bradford, Youngstown, Akron, Wheeling, Zanesville, Dayton, and Cleveland, where Bette Davis was out front; it was rumored that she would be playing Regina in the movie version, instead of Tallulah. Fort Wayne and St. Louis, where John Emery [Miss Bankhead's husband], on tour with Gertrude Lawrence in *Skylark*, joined Tallulah and Eugenia Rawls for drinks and a movie. Decatur, Danville, Champaign, Peoria, South Bend, Joliet, and Milwaukee. In Milwaukee, some ladies in the audience started screaming "Fire! Fire!" Stepping out of her character as Regina but in Regina's sharpest voice, Tallulah hissed, "Ladies! This is ridiculous. Go back to your seats. There is no fire." She did not learn until after the show that it had indeed been an imaginary whiff of smoke that had led the ladies to panic. The ladies had gone back to their seats; the show had gone on. In Madison, a blizzard was raging, and Tallulah was told that no trains would be able to leave the city that night. Tallulah: "Put on your biggest snow-plow. If necessary, my company and I will push!" The train took off on schedule. Reaching St. Paul, they found it snowbound. Only thirteen people were in the auditorium where *The Little Foxes* was to play. Tallulah: "If they could get here, we can play!" Cedar Rapids, Davenport, Des Moines, Sioux City, Omaha, Kansas City, Wichita, Colorado Springs. Tallulah charged Eugenia with waking her in time to catch a glimpse of Pike's Peak. Having been waked, she stared at it for a moment, said "All right," and went back to sleep. Denver, Salt Lake City, Butte, Helena, Missoula, Spokane, Seattle. Eugenia fell ill, and Tallulah sent for a doctor. . . . The illness was diagnosed as exhaustion, and Tallulah set about nursing Eugenia back to health. She was invited to share Tallulah's suite at the hotel in Tacoma. Tallulah had opened her bedroom windows wide before going to bed; next day, snow lay in drifts over the carpeted floor. Tallulah called room service and ordered breakfast, then added: "And please send someone to shovel the snow." In San Francisco, Eugenia and Donald Seawell announced their engagement backstage, and on Christmas Eve Tallulah gave them an engagement party. . . .

The Little Foxes company made its way slowly back across the country and ended the tour in Philadelphia, on April 5, 1941. Eugenia and Donald were married that morning, with Tallulah acting as their matron of honor and presiding over their wedding breakfast. . . . The last performance of The Little Foxes was given that evening. The orchestra played "Auld Lang Syne" and the company joined hands and sang along with the audience. They had been on the road for many months, in all weathers and under the pressure of an intolerable schedule, and Tallulah had not missed a single performance.

BRENDAN GILL
Tallulah, 1972

Many years after her retirement from the stage, Katharine Cornell remains one of the best loved stars in the American theater. During her career she combined beauty and talent with a warm and humble personality that influenced not only the audience but members of her company as well. The playwright S.N. Behrman had an opportunity to observe the actress closely during her appearance in No Time for Comedy, *as this entry from his diary indicates.*

No Time for Comedy was the third production of the Playwrights' Company. I sent the final draft to Bob Sherwood before I had even become a member. He was keen about it. He said Katharine Cornell would be great for it, and undertook to get her for me as well as her husband, Guthrie McClintic, to direct. . . . Miss Cornell was the most popular star in the country; an emanation of her rich and generous personality, as well as her luminous beauty, had gotten across to the American audience. In the course of the two-year run of my play I got to know her well. Exhibitionism is taken for granted as the sine qua non ingredient in any acting career; Miss Cornell had less of it than any actress or actor I have ever known. Her position in the theatre transcended technique; she was not, like Ina Claire and Lynn Fontanne, a great comedienne. It was something essential in herself, as a person, that the audiences sensed and reached out to. Had she not been an actress, she might have been the effective head of a great humanitarian enterprise. Once, in Boston, at the Wilbur Theatre, I peeped at the stage through the closed auditorium doors. I could hear nothing but I saw Miss Cornell. I became instantly aware that the whole stage and the other actors took light from the radiance of her personality.

Who to get to play opposite her? Harold Freedman, who knew all the great actors as well as those who were to become great, called up young Laurence Olivier, who was then in Hollywood. He sent him the script; Larry consented to play the part. Once we had Cornell and Olivier, Guthrie was able to complete the casting most felicitously. We had, besides Larry, two other Englishmen, Robert Flemyng and John

Williams. Flemyng played the tiny part of Pym. Lynn Fontanne once told me that Pym was the best small part she had ever read. No member of the audience knew at the end of the play what a tiny part it was; Flemyng had made it salient. We had Margalo Gillmore, who had been in my first play, and whose satiric humor had cheered me up often during the intervening years; and Gee Gee James, who played the maid. We embarked by train for Indianapolis, where we were to open. . . .

We opened, appropriately enough, at the English Theatre, a lovely old house which reminded me of the Hollis in Boston. It must have been of about the same vintage and has probably disappeared by now, as the Hollis has. Because Kit was in the play the performances were all sold out before we arrived. Bob Sherwood and the rest of my colleagues showed up, as did Alexander Woollcott, a devoted friend of Kit's. The little contingent from New York did not alleviate the tension of appearing before a new audience; if anything, it heightened it. It was apparent to me, from the first, that Kit was nervous and insecure; it was the first time in years that she had played a straight comedy part. John Williams, who had a long scene with Kit, before Larry came on, played with authority and ease and made his effect in a strange laconic part. Larry walked on in his street suit. His playing was, from the moment of his entrance, so effulgent that the audience was startled and fascinated. Kit looked wonderful; she had her beauty, but beauty is a static thing. Larry had the most engaging and volatile good looks. There was a stir in the audience about him that lasted all evening. His authority and idiosyncrasy were so compelling that it put the play out of balance in a way; the other actors seemed a bit perfunctory. The only one who was imperturbable was Bobby Flemyng as Pym; he had a razorlike edge to his comedy-playing that nothing could dent. In the intermissions I heard people exchanging queries about who this surprising young man Olivier was and where had he been keeping himself all this time. When it was over I went to see Kit in her dressing room. She was crying.

"I let you down," she said.

I made light of it. "Bob and the others," I said, "think the play got over."

"Thanks to Larry," she said.

In our conference after the play, at which Aleck Woollcott put in an appearance to register how dazzled he was by Larry, I was conscious of the panic that afflicts managements on occasions like this: "Would Kit quit?" But the apprehensive ones did not know Kit. She did not quit. She stuck. She got better and better as she vanquished her nervousness. The company was her responsibility. She mothered it. They all blossomed under her ministrations. I made a discovery myself: the woman she was playing *was* Kit, though I had hardly known her when I wrote the part. She became surer and surer. By the time the company left Indianapolis it was an ensemble. . . .

In New York Brooks Atkinson wrote: "The cast is the most spring-like event that a sullen April has borne this season." Of Kit he said: "After two years of silence in New York, which does not enjoy the quiet, Katharine Cornell has returned in all her magnificence, playing comedy with effortless skill and personal sincerity." The company settled down happily for a run at the Ethel Barrymore Theatre. I have never known anything quite like the sympathy and warmth of that engagement. . . .

. . . The evening I got back [from a trip to London] I looked in at the Ethel Barrymore. Everything was going tidily. But when I went back to see Kit, I found her downcast. She told me awful news: Olivier was leaving. . . . He promised to stay to the end of the New York run. But he simply could not remain for the transcontinental tour that Guthrie had arranged for the following fall and winter. It was a heavy blow. When it became apparent that England would soon be at war, Bobby Flemyng left too. . . .

There were two doleful evenings when I went to see Bobby Flemyng for the last time and Larry for the last time. I went with Gertrude Macy, Kit's business manager and a great buddy of mine. Gert Macy was considered one of the ablest managers in New York. On both occasions Flemyng and Larry were at their best, which made the evenings more poignant. I condoled with Gert—she felt the way I did. Gert and I took Kit home. We mourned Larry. "It was so exciting playing with him," Kit said. "You never could tell what he would do. But whatever he did it was always right—some new facet, some new insight." When we left Kit, I said to Gert that I couldn't imagine the play without Larry but that Kit had to do more than imagine it: she had to play it. "That is exactly what she will do," said Gert. "She will play it. Moreover, she will keep it up. You'll see!"

Play it Kit did, till late next spring, on an immense tour that went from Boston to Seattle, with major cities in between, and from Seattle south through California and Texas, to New Orleans; from New Orleans north through the East to the final performance in Newark. From Newark I went to Kit's house where she was giving a farewell party for the company.

. . . Everyone was pretty tired; the company had been touring hard for many months. Guthrie made a little speech and gave me a present from the company, a silver cigarette box with a map of the United States on the cover with a red band marking every town the company had played. Gee Gee James, John Williams and Margalo, the veteran elite of the original company, stood around the piano and sang. The stage manager played the piano. It was all slow-paced and pleasant. I sat with Kit on a sofa in a corner, under a Burchfield painting. I thanked Kit for what she had done for me and for the play.

"The audiences enjoyed it," she said, "but I was never, not from the beginning, happy about my own performance. I have never been happy about my own performance—not in anything!"

I said that was nonsense, that she had been marvelous in *The Barretts of Wimpole Street.*

"I came nearest in that," she said. "That suited me. But you know ..." She paused; she was gathering her thoughts. "I wanted to act when I was young. There was nothing I wanted so much. But I was never secure in it. I never ..." She paused again. "I've always had to be cautious."

S.N. BEHRMAN
People in a Diary, 1972

Bert Lahr was one of the last great clowns of Broadway. He shone in musical comedies and revues such as Flying High, Hold Everything, *and* Du Barry Was a Lady. *Later, when changing styles brought an end to that type of musical theater, Lahr turned to more dramatic roles—most memorably as Estragon in* Waiting for Godot. *But slapstick comedy was his forte, as we see through the eyes of his son, drama critic John Lahr, who describes Lahr's performance in* The Beauty Part.

Bert Lahr in The Beauty Part

Bert Lahr stands alone in the wings waiting for his cue. He wears a smoking jacket with a shawl wrapped formally around his shoulders. A woolen beanie is pulled down to his eyebrows. It is damp in the backstage darkness; linoleum muffles every step. Bert Lahr seems to blend into the dusty shadows. There is nothing in his manner or in his worn face that indicates success. And yet, in that body, dwarfed beside the stage house, is a humor that has weathered five decades of drastic shifts in American comic taste.

He waits patiently, looking continually at his feet or the leathery, freckled skin of his hands. From the wings, the sense of isolation that surrounds his craft is unmistakable. The heads of the audience jutt out from their seats like bleached rock faces, detached from their bodies. The glare of the stage lights blurs their identities.

This is my father's world, and where he comes mysteriously alive. The scene is the creation of S. J. Perelman; but the character, Nelson Smedley, aged ice-cream tycoon, becomes Lahr's unique invention. He can never be certain how the character evolved. "I just play in it; then it's almost intuitive."

His cue comes. He moves from the shadows into the white light of center stage, and the transformation is immediate and complete. His body finds new rhythms. His legs, pale and spindly at home, churn with furious energy. His fingers, delicate and langorous off stage, lash out, discovering the violence of senility.

"Get your paws off me! I can walk as good as the next man!" Nelson Smedley casts off his nurse, begins to take his first steps, and topples to the floor. The audience roars in response.

"Pushed me again, didn't you? Always pushing—push, push, push, puuuuuussssssh!"

To the audience, he is a slick professional—smooth, direct, with impeccable timing. They have always laughed at my father. They joke about his face—full of crags and mysterious angles, with a nose swollen like a gherkin. Even his eyes, penetrating and deep-set beads, can be manipulated into something outrageous. From the wings, his buffoonery, at sixty-eight, seems a much more personal and painful struggle than he allows anyone, even himself, to believe. If he rarely ventures outside his apartment, on stage he takes immense physical and emotional risks. He falls; his body unravels in flurries of contorted movement. The pratfall becomes the flesh's humiliation, and its redemption is laughter. The activity is hypnotic and strangely ugly; what is referred to so matter-of-factly at home as "business" becomes disciplined and controlled art. The gales of laughter that greet Nelson Smedley are not so much the product of the dialogue as of the gymnastics of his face, the bellowing and the slapstick antics that expand the words.

Lahr howls at the audience. The spittle from his slurred words sprays out against the darker background of the mezzanine. He has howled in his own way off and on the stage for many years. Gnashing his teeth, shivering in Smedley's paranoic rage, he crouches toward the audience, screaming. "Stop thief! Stop thieieieiefff!!" The noise is not rational. It leaps from his stomach like an animal's screech. Words are reduced to frequencies of fear. Like his theatrical trademark—"Gnong, gnong, gnong"—experience merges into a private language, a random conjunction of gutteral expressions. This never happens at home. The effect on an audience is magnetic.

At the finale, Lahr moves off to a volley of applause. As he comes toward me his heavy make-up shines with sweat; his costume is gray with it.

"It went well tonight, Pop."

JOHN LAHR
Notes on a Cowardly Lion, 1969

Throughout her long and distinguished theatrical career Helen Hayes undertook many challenging roles, but none seemed more difficult— yet ultimately proved more triumphant—than her portrayal of Queen Victoria in Laurence Housman's Victoria Regina.

When Gilbert Miller sent me *Victoria Regina* by Laurence Housman, I let the manuscript lie around for weeks without giving it notice. Those two words on the title page frightened and crushed me. *Victoria Regina*—it sounded so pompous, it sounded like everything that I didn't want to get mixed up in. During that time a friend asked me what I was reading for next season. I told him that Gilbert had sent me *Victoria Regina.* He looked at me and said, "What does that mean?" and when I replied, "Queen Victoria," he said, "Oh, how dark brown!" And this is the way I felt. Then one day Gilbert called and asked,

"Have you read it—if you haven't you must at once because I'm going to lose my rights to this. There's some kind of hassle going on and it's imperative that you read it."

Indeed, I had been rude to a dear and trusted friend. So I picked it up and since it was spring and a beautiful day I went out into the garden to read it. I was sitting there, reading the play, when I heard the voices of neighbors, some Nyack ladies coming down to view the garden. I had gotten about half through the manuscript and had become riveted to it. I was so scared that my visitors would break this tremendous rapport between me and my play that I looked around wildly for a place to hide. There is a little bathhouse at the end of our swimming pool—it's very dark, a little wooden thing that's pretty enough on the outside but it sure isn't a place in which to sit cozily and read a play. But I dashed into that because I couldn't make it up to the house without running into those women. And I huddled there. I could hear their voices saying to the gardener, "Where is Mrs. MacArthur?" and so on. And the poor gardener, who had not seen my retreat, kept saying incredulously, "Well, Mrs. MacArthur was here a minute ago." And so, locked in that little bathhouse, sitting there on the floor because there is no chair in there, I finished *Victoria Regina*. Everything about the play seemed so wonderful. . . .

As I have said, I loved the play and agreed to do it. But I was scared of doing the old queen. I didn't know how to play that kind of old lady. She was rather fat and pompous and choleric in the last scenes. There were thirty-two vignettes in the original script, and, of these, nine had been selected to be performed, the last three dealing with the aging queen. I just couldn't conceive of being able to play those scenes. Consequently I convinced myself that the play really ended with Albert's death and that it would really be wrong to continue after that. I said to myself this was the love story of a little German princess and she had a fine German prince and we mustn't try to make anything else out of it. Of course I was wrong in every way. But at the time I was aflame with conviction and I spoke to Gilbert Miller about it. He shrugged and said, "If you feel that way, maybe it would be better if you talked to Housman."

Maybe Gilbert knew what he was doing when he agreed to pay my expenses to England to see Housman. I never met such a bullheaded person in my life. Thank goodness he was. When I argued that the play should end with Albert's death because that was the end of the great love story, and that was what the whole play was about and the rest was just tacked on, he wouldn't even discuss it with me. Those last scenes were his reason for writing the play. He brushed me aside. The play had to be done with them or not at all. He behaved like an old bully, a road-company Shaw. So back home I went, defeated and desperate.

Through the rehearsal period I struggled with the old queen. We were playing in Baltimore and I still had not found her. I was awful, like an amateur in a high-school production. I didn't know what to do. I was in a panic, blinded and confused. Then it happened. One night, as I lay in bed my Graddy Hayes marched across my vision. There she was and there was Victoria. She settled down inside of me and took over. My Grandmother Hayes had been a devotee of Victoria. When I was a child, she used to describe Victoria's wedding procession. She had been in the crowd on the curb in London to cheer as the Queen went by. Later, as an old lady, she began to affect the style of Queen Victoria. The Queen died when I was a year old, but for ten years after that my grandmother wore the bonnet with the black egret that was high Victorian fashion, and conducted herself like her idol. I couldn't dissociate Victoria Regina in her scenes as the old lady from my Grandmother Hayes. I never saw anything but my Graddy in my mind's eye every night I played the part. And that was more than a thousand times.

HELEN HAYES
A Gift of Joy, 1955

Helen Hayes in Victoria Regina

Laurette Taylor's career in the theater spanned four decades. Beginning with the 1912 production of Peg O' My Heart, *Miss Taylor and her husband, playwright-director J. Hartley Manners, kept Broadway audiences entertained with a succession of romantic comedies and dramas. But Manners' death in 1928 nearly destroyed Laurette, and for more than ten years she wallowed in an alcoholic haze, squandering her talent. But in a manner that rivals many fictitious stories about theatrical comebacks, Laurette returned to the stage as Mrs. Midget in Otto Preminger's revival of* Outward Bound.

It was like the old days with Hartley. Their views on acting were amazingly similar, the Viennese-trained director, and the melodrama-trained Laurette. "She had an uncanny ability to put her finger on a central weakness of another actor," Preminger recalled, "and she could be very sharp about it." Then he added with a smile, "She was not in any sense a mild woman." As to her drinking: "It would have been quite hopeless to approach her with a promise-me-you'll-be-a-good-girl technique. There was a demon in her that would not be boxed like that. It was in part what made her so weird on the stage—surprising you with unexpected phrasing and accent; the fluid, the unexpected, this was the nub of her inspiration. To approach her with a program of being good, of never touching another drop, was to try and box her demon. She would never allow it. I knew this at once."

Laurette called him M'sieur Printemps, kidded him about his still heavy Viennese accent, imitated the wiggle of his fingers over his head when he grew excited about some new idea. She was happy again. The theatre was as it had been in the days long ago. . . .

As the day of the opening approached Laurette seemed confident and untroubled. At dress rehearsal she was satisfied to see that the mechanics of the part were right without giving a performance. Eloise [Sheldon], at the theatre each day helping Bramwell Fletcher with incidental producing chores, had yet to feel the full power of Laurette's genius. So, for that matter, had Preminger.

The day of the opening he called an early rehearsal and kept the company at the theatre most of the day. Laurette protested; Hartley never had more than a line rehearsal in the morning and dismissed the company. Preminger considered this gravely. "I think it is better we do it this way," he said quietly. Fletcher had several tasks for Eloise outside the theatre but she refused to go. "You can fire me if you want to," she said, "but I'm not going to leave Laurette." At five o'clock the company was dismissed for supper. Laurette and Eloise had been going to and from rehearsals in the subway to save money, but Laurette considered this occasion sufficiently momentous to throw caution to the winds. "This time we take a taxi," she announced; "my luck can't be bad forever."

By the time they were home she was sick with nerves, but dined well on rare steak as Hartley had taught her. The tension, she told Eloise, was not because of any doubts about herself but a reflection of the tension she anticipated on the other side of the footlights as to whether she would go through, and the worry lest this tension affect the other actors. By the time her make-up was on, however, she was calm.

In pork-pie hat, black alpaca cape and tippet of fur, holding a capacious knitting bag, Laurette made her entrance backing cautiously through stage door left. Most of the cast was assembled onstage and had received their hand. On sight of the nondescript little figure sidling backwards through the door the audience burst into thunderous applause. Laurette turned to say her first lines but it was of no use. The ovation continued, gathering momentum. People shouted and whistled and wept; they beat their feet on the floor; here and there groups rose, until finally the whole audience was standing. The humble shawl-wrapped figure bent a little at one knee, thrust one high-buttoned shoe tentatively forward, then drew it back. The hands with the knitting bag fluttered uncertainly up to the throat and down again. Still the demonstration went on. It was obvious that Laurette was shaken—shattered, almost—by the prolonged ovation, but also evident was the delicate poise, the established inner equilibrium of the artist that cannot be swayed by emotional turmoil within or without. She tried to stop them in every way she knew how; she fumbled with the cheap handles of the knitting bag, swung it down at her side, pressed it high over her heart; her hands moved in small patterns of humility and service, essentially the gestures of Mrs. Midget. But it was hopeless. A floodgate of welcome and homage and rejoicing had opened and the audience would not, could not, stop. For ten solid minutes shock waves of sound buffeted the tiny figure on the stage.

Somehow, finally, Laurette managed to say her first line, then quickly moved to a chair, plunked herself down, drew two large knitting needles from the bag and began to knit. It was a gesture both humble and commanding, humorous and apologetic. The tender and moving quality of it reached out like a quieting hand and drew the audience ever so gently under the spell of the self-effacing Mrs. Midget.

At the end of the play there were twenty-two curtain calls and Laurette made three grateful little speeches; not much, just murmurs between the thunderous acclaim. Several times she held her hand over her mouth as though trying not to shout back, the incredible brows arching high with excitement. There was no false humility, but pride and gratitude and a kind of shared astonishment on her face, as though she said to her audience as she stood there looking out, "Yes, the truth is wonderful, isn't it? The most wonderful thing in the world! It was in me all this time. I'm glad I could bring it to you again." And beneath her artist's pride her heart was melting with the warmth of the affection that came flooding across the footlights. They remembered. They cared. They loved her. The metamorphosis was complete.

Afterward, in direct contrast with the stream of wellwishers backstage, emotion overcame her. Putting her arms around Theresa Helburn, Laurette wept, "Oh, Terry—it's back! The theatre's back!" Later, walking to their home for supper arm in arm with Vincent Price and his wife the lovely Edith Barrett, she said, "It really wasn't a very good performance." Still not humility; just a bob curtsy to that inner vision, not quite lived up to under the unusual stresses of the evening.

MARGUERITE COURTNEY
Laurette, 1955

When Oklahoma! *opened on Broadway in 1943 it marked a considerable breakthrough in the development of musical theater. In their first collaboration Richard Rodgers and Oscar Hammerstein discarded virtually the entire roster of musical comedy conventions—and replaced them with lovely songs skillfully integrated in a gentle, warm-hearted play. The phenomenal success that* Oklahoma! *has enjoyed over the years more than justifies the faith that the Theatre Guild and its directors—led by Lawrence Langner and Theresa Helburn—placed in this "risky experiment."*

The book of *Oklahoma!* was completed in the late summer of 1942, and all through the fall and winter thereafter, we held auditions in the Guild Theatre for singers and actors. It was soon decided that Alfred Drake . . . would make a good Curly, and Joan Roberts . . . was selected as Laurey. While we were auditioning actors and actresses for these roles, we were also engaged in financing the musical. As our own treasury [the Theatre Guild's] was so depleted, it was obvious that we could not produce *Oklahoma!* without outside capital. . . .

. . . We decided the best way to do this would be to have Dick, Oscar, Alfred Drake and Joan Roberts attend a number of tea parties or cocktail parties to which prospective backers would be invited, and then to play and sing the songs to them so that they would not be buying a pig in a poke. . . .

While *Oklahoma!* was in rehearsal at the Guild Theatre, Oscar and Dick were writing new songs without any apparent effort during the rehearsals . . . Terry [Helburn] and John Gassner, our playreader, suggested that some kind of rousing song of the earth would be helpful in the second act, and one day Dick and Oscar appeared at the theatre, sat at the piano where we surrounded them on benches and chairs, while they played for us the rousing melody of the song "Oklahoma!". . . .

After the dress rehearsal, there were a number of small adjustments, and the play opened with the title *Away We Go* on the evening of March 11, 1943, to an audience made up of New Haven play-goers, Yale students, a considerable number of New York managers, and finally the investors who came out of curiosity to learn the fate of their investment. The first half of the play flowed like a dream. . . .

The second act did not play so well, but when the final curtain fell, the play received warm applause from the audience. . . .

As the crowd of managers, backers, friends of the actors, the composer and author chatted on the stage after the play was over, a well-known musical comedy producer who seldom talks in tones quieter than a resounding shout, informed everybody present that Oscar would have to rewrite the second act completely. Another important musical comedy producer called me on the telephone the next day and spent twenty minutes arguing with me that the perverted farm hand Jud should not be killed in the second act, because, in his experience of twenty-five years of producing musical comedies, there had never been a killing in one of them! I stated gently but firmly that this was essential to the play, and we would have to let it go at that. So pessimistic were the reports that came out of New Haven regarding the second act, that we decided to sell some additional interest in the play in order to be prepared for staying out of New York longer, if that were necessary, or to take care of losses in New York. . . .

By a rearrangement of the material in the second act, and with little rewriting, within ten days of the opening of the play in Boston, it was in excellent shape, and in practically the exact condition in which it opened in New York. . . .

When we were in Boston, a musical play called *Dancing in the Streets.* . . . was playing against us, and there was quite a question as to whether we should not try to race in to New York ahead of this play. Rudolf Kommer, Max Reinhart's shadow . . . came to Boston and saw both *Oklahoma!* and *Dancing in the Streets*, and he was as loud in his praises of the latter as he was pessimistic about the fate of *Oklahoma!* I myself had been worried as to what would happen in New York,

Playbill for the original production of Oklahoma!

because *Oklahoma!* was so different from any of the musicals which were running at the time. . . .

When the fateful day arrived for the opening of *Oklahoma!* in New York, we refused to allow anyone to be seated during the singing of the opening number, "Oh, What a Beautiful Morning," and it was apparent to me from the beginning of the play that it had started off on the right foot. I wondered how a New York audience would respond to the fact that for nearly forty-five minutes, not a single chorus girl appeared on the stage. But as one beautiful song followed another, the audience took the play to its heart, and there was the most tremendous outburst of applause at the end of the ballet, as the curtain fell upon the first act. During the intermission, I noted there was that electric thrill which passes through an audience when it feels that it is attending something of exciting import in the theatre.

During the second act, after the gaiety of the "Cowman and the Farmer" songs and dances, there was no doubt about the outcome. At the end of the play, the applause was overwhelming . . . the next day the newspaper critics wrote column upon column of praise for Rodgers, Hammerstein, Mamoulian [director] and De Mille [choreographer]; there was not a single bad newspaper notice. And then the legend of *Oklahoma!* began to grow.

LAWRENCE LANGNER
The Magic Curtain, 1951

One of the most memorable Shakespearean productions ever to appear on Broadway was Margaret Webster's Othello. *Paul Robeson, the renowned black singer and actor, was cast in the lead—with Jose Ferrer as Iago, Uta Hagen (then Mrs. Ferrer) as Desdemona, and Miss Webster as Emilia. The noted director recalled the long, trying road to opening night in her autobiography.*

The rehearsals for the summer-stock production were hard for me. Officially we had only two weeks, one in New York; but the Ferrers, Paul and I had worked on the play long before that. I had decided to play Emilia myself. At first this made things easier, since during the New York rehearsal week we were only allowed three other actors besides the Ferrers and Robeson. Later it confronted me with hazards, as I well knew it would. I have never been much in favor of the director acting in his own show. It used to be widely done; now much more rarely. I don't really like doing it myself, especially when the play is one of depth and stature. I don't believe my work as a director suffers; with a good technical staff and a reliable understudy, the rehearsal stages can be well covered; but my acting does. I find it very difficult to close my directorial eyes and ears and to become subjective, immersed, spontaneous. . . .

Above all, I was engaged in a task which today sounds ludicrously

Paul Robeson in Othello

unnecessary: that of proving in print, on the air, through press interviews and by every known propaganda means, that Othello was really intended to be a black man from Africa, not a coffee-colored gentleman who has been spending the winter in Tunisia. I did this with conviction because I myself believe it. But I found that you could make a perfectly good case for anything you wanted to prove merely by selecting your favored commentator. "Tawny" says one scholar decisively; "black" snaps another without hesitation. "A half-caste" describes Fechter's famous rendering; "an animal, tropical black" decides a fourth. Edmund Kean broke away from the original "black" tradition by presenting a pale, cafe-au-lait Othello—"a most pleasing probability," said Coleridge; but Shakespeare's own Burbage, poor simple man, seems to have played just what the text says—"black"; "begrimed and black"; "sooty bosom"; "thick lips" and all. With this, of course, I made much play; also using as targets the more ludicrous of the coffee-colored brigade through such quotes as this, from Miss Mary Preston of Maryland in 1869: "We may regard, then, the daub of black upon Othello's visage as an EBULLITION of fancy, a FREAK of imagination—one of the few erroneous strokes of the great master's brush. Othello was a WHITE man." . . .

The opening night in Cambridge was about the hottest I ever remember. The small theatre had a corrugated-iron roof and was packed to its girders with sweating humanity. We sweated even more from nerves and also because we were all encased in velvet gowns, heavy cloaks, leather thigh boots and so on. Paul's robes had to be wrung out between scenes. The tension added to the heat. But when the final curtain fell, the audience cheered and clapped and roared, accompanied by a steady, rhythmic stamping of feet. "What's that?" I asked the man beside me, one of the local actors. "Boy!" said he, "that's Harvard! that's the best you could get!" Within twenty-four hours the telephones were red-hot with all the New York managers who had turned us down asking for "a piece of the show."

It was a year before we were able to open there, however, because of Paul's intervening concert commitments. After much discussion it was agreed that the Theatre Guild should "present" the show, finance it and control all the "front of the house" part; but that the production itself should be in the hands of a trio consisting of Robeson, our production stage manager and myself. We got Bobby Jones to do the sets and costumes. He took infinite trouble to choose for Paul fabrics and colors which would suit him, and to have them cut to his best advantage. The sets were simple and swift to change, but they had the richness and line characteristic of Jones's best work.

The Ferrers stayed with us, Joe's performance improving all the time. Uta lost a little of her first, spontaneous simplicity—the hardest thing to retain or recapture. Paul grew in confidence through the rehearsals and try-out weeks; but he would keep fiddling around with an electronic gadget which was supposed to hang in the auditorium and echo back his voice so that he would "hear himself." This harassed the rest of us and took weeks to banish. The try-out dates were fine; but I knew very well that an out-of-town triumph doesn't at all preclude destruction by the New York press, and was not lulled into a false security. Came the opening at the Shubert, October 19, 1943.

I have never been so paralytic with fright. Director's nerves, which are the worst kind; actor's nerves—including the two minutes of pure agony just before you step on the stage; the accumulated pressure of the past four years; and the menacing awareness that the issues were larger than theatre-size. I didn't listen to the opening scenes; I tried to blot out everything but Emilia. Jauntily, I landed with Uta at Cyprus. I hadn't been on the stage two minutes before I knew for certain that it was going to be all right.

There is, perhaps, only one thing which totally distinguishes the stage from its mechanical competitors—the live communication between living actors and a living audience. When the electric spark leaps from the stage to the auditorium, when the pressure mounts till the needle almost runs off the gauge, the theatre could quite easily explode. Bobby Jones said of the *Othello* opening, "If a cat had walked across the footlights it would have been electrocuted."

In cold blood, I think the performance that night could be ranked as "good." We gave others just as good or better; but that night "the spirit gave us utterance"—or maybe it rested on the audience: in either case, it was, I still think, the most exciting evening I have ever experienced in the theatre. When, as Emilia, I finally "died," I lay on the floor (back to the audience, of course) helpless to move a muscle, with the tears running down my face. Someone has rightly said that it isn't losing the race which makes you cry, it's winning it.

There followed an ovation worthy of one of today's Pop singers, lasting twenty minutes, all of us in a pool of tears, yells for a "speech," all of us speechless, a final choky "thank you" from me, and the next morning's adjectives: "unbelievably magnificent," "terrific," "consummate genius," "one of the great events of theatre history," and a line at the box office as soon as it opened. I wrote a note of congratulations and thanks and put it up on the call board. I added: "We have set ourselves a terrific standard . . . but . . . There's nothing about it we cannot retain and surpass . . ." I hope we did.

Margaret Webster
Don't Put Your Daughter on the Stage, 1972

One casualty of shifting audience tastes in the early twentieth century was the burlesque show. Among those who mourned this passing form of entertainment was the drama critic George Jean Nathan.

One of the most depressing changes that has come about in the American theatre in our time is the gradual passing out of the old-time burlesque show, erstwhile delight of all connoisseurs of humour in its jock-strap. With the Columbia Wheel presently going in for revivals of *Uncle Tom's Cabin* and productions of such past Broadway successes as *White Cargo*, with police injunctions to managers of such houses as the Chelsea either to behave or to shut up shop, and with the authorities of the Mutual Wheel toning down their exhibitions until they are indistinguishable from so many Epworth League picnics, the burlesque show as we knew it twenty years ago seems doomed to go the way of such other estimable American institutions as cock fights, rye whisky, and liberty.

The signs of the death of burlesque have been in the air these last ten years and more. It was at about that time that the two-hundred-pound blondes whom once we frantically cheered began to send in coupons out of the backs of the magazines asking for free samples of reducing cream, that the sons of the late lamented house managers, succeeding to their fathers' posts after four years at Harvard, began to look askance at the scene in which Ludwig Dinkeplatz besought Hyman Finkelstein to take his feet out of the soup, and that the producers of the shows got rid of the old backdrop representing the Casino at Monte Carlo, a lovable standby since the Civil War, and bought in its place a secondhand set of scenery from the Casino at Broadway and Thirty-ninth Street. It was also at this time that the burlesque entrepreneurs began to feel the first faint symptoms of morality and to wrinkle their brows over the scene in which the Irish comedian inquired ironically of Babe La Gervaise, the prima donna, why she wore her bustle in her shirtwaist, and why she wore two of them.

Up to this period, burlesque had been untrammeled and carefree. It was as left alone as a pretzel in Paris. And it flourished to the delight of all and sundry. Then came the first ripples of the blue waves that were presently to drown it, along with so many other things that once brought happiness to the humble American. Today it is but a ghost of its former self, and that ghost is yearly getting more shadowy. Soon it will vanish completely. On the stage where once we boys applauded the spectacle of the great Al Reeves pointing to a blonde hippopotamus and asking if anyone in the audience would give him a quarter for her, provided he threw in his hat, there will be only a tenth-rate performance of some stale tenth-rate Broadway play. On the stage that once held *Krausmeyer's Alley*, upon which no less that seven Presidents of the United States were fed in their youth, we shall hear nothing but the prayers of Little Eva. On the stage that once gave us, to our eternal joy, the money-changing act, the scene in which the German and Hebrew comedians pretended to be waiters in order to fool their wives, and the scene wherein the Irish comedian got an eyeful of flour when he talked into the telephone, we shall see nothing but a belated copy of the totem-pole number out of *Rose Marie* and an imitation of the Tiller Girls.

Not long ago, in the burlesque house down in Fourteenth Street, I actually saw two sailors and a pickpocket break down and cry like children over the passing of the old order. The Hebrew comedian, instead of stealing up on the cooch dancer and jocosely belaboring her rear with a large bologna sausage, as in the happy days of the McKinley era, simply sidled nervously around her for a moment or two and made his exit. The Irish comique, instead of leaning under the table to get a better view of the soubrette's ample limb and falling on his nose as a result, simply went into a tame song and dance with the lady. And the German funny man, instead of sitting on the elephantine prima donna's lap and dropping nickels down her decollete, approached the fair creature gingerly and bestowed a peck upon her shoulder blade. To those of us who have the best interests of the native drama at heart and are willing to lay down our lives that the honor and integrity of the American theatre may be preserved, it was all too awful.

Speaking for the generation of the early nineties, I urge upon the burlesque impresarios a reconsideration of their present devastating and highly obnoxious plans. Let them give back to us Billy Watson in all his glory, together with the Heinies and Izzies and Mikes of blessed memory. Let them bring back, without delay, the old fat girls, the old floppy breeches, and old red undershirts, and old suspenders made of rope, the old green vests, the old Limburger-cheese jokes, the old backdrop of Union Square, and the old scene in which the fierce-looking cop who cowed the comedians turned out to be a lizzie. Then again all of us Shakespeare and Ibsen enthusiasts will be happy.

GEORGE JEAN NATHAN
The Art of Night, 1928

Although Walter Kerr is best known as a distinguished drama critic—currently writing each Sunday for The New York Times—*he has also been associated with the theater as a producer, a director, and also as the husband of the successful playwright Jean Kerr. Thus, his observations on the feverish manipulations that affect all shows being readied for a Broadway opening are not merely those of a detached spectator, but the sometimes painful memories of one who has been on the firing line himself in such pre-Broadway stops as Washington, D.C., Philadelphia, Boston, and New Haven.*

The people who empty wastebaskets in New Haven have a terrible time of it during these early weeks. With a whole squadron of productions hurling themselves at the out-of-town firing lines, hoping to survive for what always looks like a lush October in New York, the period of cutting and hacking and wholesale rewriting begins.

Into the trash cans of Philadelphia and Boston go entire scenes, once cherished characters, long speeches the author truly loved, and thousands of odd snippets that have—under the chillingly accurate eye of an actual audience—become spectacularly superfluous. Subordinate figures that were written as males turn, in the twist of a typewriter, into females; where two noble souls once threaded their ways through the labyrinth of an author's plotting, one composite soul now strides the stage on sturdier, or perhaps wobblier, legs; an ingenue who has spent her rehearsal time finding true love in the arms of a swarthy juvenile discovers, after the first week's run, that her heart was quite misplaced and that the curtain is hereafter going to come down on her passionate acceptance of the elderly roué who was so funny in the first and second acts. Life is malleable in the theatrical suburbs. . . .

And absurdity is very often the result of those frantic late-night decisions in cluttered hotel rooms, decisions arrived at under the pressure of mounting financial losses, the increasing tremors of a star facing disaster in New York, and the joint bafflement of authors, directors, and producers who had imagined they were creating one kind of play and are now being told by intelligent customers that they have hatched quite another. . . . Even obvious successes, doing capacity business on the journey into town, are apt to take weekly losses here. The costs of repainting a piece of furniture that a backer's wife doesn't like, relighting an alcove that the star's agent doesn't like, and restaging a scene that even the author's mother doesn't like are so high that possible profits are quickly gobbled up in the desperate determination to make a going thing go better. The rumble of thunder is always overhead.

I doubt, though, that much real harm is done. When a show comes into New York with the leading character suffering from sunstroke rather than her original sinus condition, or with the principal comedian doing his old vaude routine to make up for a certain lack in the second act, the chances are about a thousand to one that the enterprise wasn't exactly a pip to begin with. I am reliably informed that a musical to which we were treated not long ago was actually worse when it opened on Broadway than it had been six weeks earlier and a thousand miles away; but since it seems to have had only about a forty per cent protein content when it first saw the light of night, the reduction to thirty was not a serious loss. It is the transparently failing show that is likely to make the most frantic forays into left field. . . .

The pressure itself, exhausting as it is to the folk who are fretting under it, sometimes serves as a supercharge. Complacency is less productive than concern. And, in the end, we've always got to remember that the theater is, for good or ill, a social situation. If the paying guests don't respond as a writer meant them to respond, they can't really be told to stand in a corner and hang their heads. The writer has simply got to trot out something to keep the party going, whether it is an improved soliloquy or a passel of dancing girls.

What is going into those September wastebaskets, then, is an audience's boredom. And what comes coiling out of those hot New Haven typewriters is—sometimes—inspiration.

WALTER KERR
Pieces at Eight, 1952

A Chronology of Theater

Birth in Athens of Thespis, the first tragic poet	560 B.C.	Pisistratus becomes ruler of Athens; Greek towns of Asia Minor fall under Persian power
	551-479	Confucius teaches in China
Pisistratus organizes the Dionysian festivals; Thespis' *Competitors for Pelias* wins first prize for tragedy and introduces the concept of a single actor set apart from the chorus	534	
	516	Darius I leads Persian invasion of Thrace
	509	Traditional date assigned to the founding of the Roman Republic
Performance of Phrynichus' *The Capture of Miletus;* the author is fined for making the audience cry	492	
Aeschylus wins the first prize in the tragic competition at the Athens Dionysia	485	
	480	Greeks defeat Persians at Battle of Salamis
With Aeschylus' *The Persians*, a second actor is introduced	475	
Aeschylus' trilogy *Oresteia* wins the tragic competition at the Athens Dionysia	458	
Sophocles' *Antigone* introduces a third actor and increases the size of the chorus	442-41	
Euripides' *Medea* produced for the first time	431	Great Peloponnesian War begins
Presentation of Aristophanes' *The Banqueters* marks the beginning of the period of Old Comedy	427	
Sophocles completes *Oedipus Rex*	c.425	
Euripides writes *The Trojan Women* and *Electra*	415-13	
	411	Conservative political forces take control of Athens
Euripides' *Bacchae* and *Iphigenia at Aulis* presented; Aristophanes' *The Frogs*	405	
Sophocles' last play, *Oedipus at Colonus*, performed	401	
	390	Gauls invade Italy; Rome sacked and burned
Completion of the theater at Epidaurus	350	
	336-323	Reign of Alexander the Great of Macedonia, first great world conqueror
Performance of Menander's *Dyskolos* ("The Bad-tempered Man") marks the opening of the period of New Comedy	317	
Menander's masterpiece, *The Arbitration*, performed	304	
Livius Andronicus, founder of Latin drama, produces first Greek play translated into Latin	240	
	214	Great Wall of China completed
Presentation of *Pseudolus* by Plautus, master of Latin comic writing	191	
Terence's first play, *The Woman of Andros*, wins him entry into the Scipionic Circle, a group of writers subsidized by a wealthy Roman citizen	166	
The Eunuch and *Phormio* establish Terence's position as successor to Plautus	161	
	146	Rome destroys Carthage
	58-49	Gallic Wars; Julius Caesar extends boundaries of the Roman Empire to include Gaul
First stone theater built in Pompeii	55	
	44	Julius Caesar assassinated
	31	Octavian defeats Mark Antony at Actium
	27	Octavian receives title "Augustus" and is proclaimed first Roman emperor; *Pax Romana* begins
Birth in Cordoba of Seneca—philosopher, historian, and ancient Rome's greatest playwright	4	Birth of Jesus of Nazareth
Death of Seneca	A.D. 65	
	25 B.C.-A.D. 220	Eastern Han dynasty rules in China

The first millennium of the Christian era was remarkably quiescent insofar as theater was concerned. As a result, there is virtually no reliable information concerning the theater before the tenth century A.D., where this chronology resumes.

Horswitha, a Benedictine abbess in Germany, writes six plays modeled after the comedies of Terence	c. 935-1000	
	1096-1099	First Crusade
Representation d'Adam, an early Norman Mystery play by an unknown author	c.1150-70	
Jeu de St. Nicolas written by Jean Bodel—an important work in the transition between religious and secular drama; founding of Penitential movements in Italy produces narrative hymns known as *laudi*—first native Italian drama	c.1168 c.1200	Founding of Oxford University
	1204	Constantinople falls to soldiers of Fourth Crusade
Jeu de Robin et de Marion by Adam de la Halle	c.1265	
	1271-95	Journey of Marco Polo to the Orient
Appearance of the Chester Cycle, one of many series of Mystery plays performed each spring in England to celebrate the Feast of Corpus Christi	c.1300	Giotto paints frescoes in church of St. Francis
	1337	Outbreak of the Hundred Years' War
	1368	Founding of the Ming dynasty
Play of the Lord's Prayer, an early English Morality play whose author is unknown	c.1384	
	1387	Chaucer begins *Canterbury Tales*
Charles VI of France licenses the Confrérie de la Passion, a group of citizens and craftsmen, to present Mystery plays	1402	
	1415	Battle of Agincourt: English forces under Henry V defeat the French in a climactic battle of the Hundred Years' War
Mystère de Nouveau Testament by Arnoul Greban, a passion play composed of some 30,000 verses	1450	
	1453	Fall of Constantinople to the Ottoman Turks
	c.1454	Publication of the Gutenberg Bible marks the beginning of printing from movable type
First performance of the farce *Maitre Pierre Pathelin*, one of the most popular plays of the era	1470	
Favola d'Orfeo, a pastoral drama by Angelo Poliziano, reflects a new trend toward nonreligious subject matter for plays and the use of the vernacular	c.1480	Sandro Botticelli paints *Birth of Venus*
Lorenzo de' Medici writes the sacred drama *San Giovanni e Paolo*	1489	
	1492	Fall of Granada marks end of Moorish influence in Spain; Christopher Columbus sets forth on first voyage to the New World
La Céléstina, one of the most influential dramas of the early Renaissance; the author of Act I and portions of Act II is unknown, but the play was unquestionably completed by Fernando de Rojas	1500	
	1503-05	Leonardo da Vinci paints the Mona Lisa
First performance of *La Cassaria*, a comedy by Italian playwright, actor, and stage manager Lodovico Ariosto	1508	Raphael completes frescoes in the Vatican; Michelangelo begins ceiling of the Sistine Chapel
Bibiena's *Calandria* satirizes contemporary life	1513	
	1517	Martin Luther presents his "95 Theses"
Auto da barca do purgatorio, the first of a trilogy of Morality plays written by Gil Vicente, often called the founder of Portuguese drama	1517-19	
	1519-22	Magellan circumnavigates the globe
La Mandragora by Niccolò Machiavelli—the first comic masterpiece in the Italian language	1520	
Commedia dell'arte begins in northern Italy	1521	
John Rostell writes and publishes the interludes *Calisto and Meliboea* and *The Dialogue of Gentleness and Nobility*	1527	

179

John Heywood's *The Four R's*, a typical example of English court entertainment	1529	
	1532-34	François Rabelais writes *Gargantua and Pantagruel*
Nicholas Udall's *Ralph Roister Doister*, early Elizabethan play modeled after classical comedies	1533	
	1538	Titian completes the painting *Venus of Urbino*
	1543	Copernicus publishes discoveries on the nature of the solar system
Parlement de Paris bans Mystery plays, but they continue to be performed in the provinces	1548	
The Schoolboy Wandering in Paradise by Hans Sachs, a German dramatist known for his amusing Shrovetide plays	1550	
Cléopâtre Captive by Etienne Jodelle, considered the founder of French tragedy	1552	
	1558	Elizabeth I becomes queen of England
Performance of Thomas Norton and Thomas Sackville's *Gorboduc* introduces use of blank verse	1562	
Palladio designs Teatro Olimpico in Vicenza	1565	
	1570	Palladio writes *The Four Books of Architecture*
Aminta, a major pastoral drama by the Italian writer Torquato Tasso	1573	
The Theater, first permanent playhouse in England, built by James Burbage just outside London	1576	
	1579	El Greco paints *The Christ Despoiled* in Toledo
First performance of *Tamburlaine* by Christopher Marlowe; *The Spanish Tragedy* by Thomas Kyd	1587	
The Peonies Pavilion by the Chinese playwright T'ang Hsien-tsu; first performance of Marlowe's *Doctor Faustus*	1588	England turns back the Spanish Armada
	1590	Publication of Edmund Spenser's *Faerie Queen*
Henry VI, Parts I, II, and *III*, performed; first play attributed to William Shakespeare	1590-92	
Shakespeare writes *Romeo and Juliet*; following its production he writes his greatest comedies: *Much Ado About Nothing* (1598-99), *As You Like It* (1599-1600), and *Twelfth Night* (1599-1600)	1596	
	1598	Edict of Nantes grants French Protestants equal political rights with Catholics
Completion of *Julius Caesar* ushers in the period of Shakespeare's finest tragedies: *Hamlet* (1600-1), *Othello* (1604), *King Lear* (1605-6), and *Macbeth* (1606)	c.1599	
Shakespeare and other members of the Lord Chamberlain's Men form a syndicate to build and operate the Globe theater	1599	
	1603	Peter Paul Rubens paints *The Duke of Lerma*
John Marston's *The Malcontent* is performed by a company of child actors at Blackfriars, London	1604	
The Knight of the Burning Pestle written by Francis Beaumont; publication of Ben Jonson's classic comedy *Volpone*, a play first performed in 1606	1607	Performance of Monteverdi's *Orfeo*, considered the first opera
Spain's greatest playwright, Lope de Vega, publishes the treatise *The New Art of Writing Plays*	1609	
	1609-14	Johannes Kepler promulgates three fundamental laws of planetary motion
Performance of *The Tempest*, last play credited entirely to Shakespeare	1611-12	
Publication of John Webster's tragedy *The White Devil*, which precedes *The Duchess of Malfi*	1612	
	1613	Michael Romanov ascends the Russian throne, establishing a dynasty that endures until 1917
	1615	Cervantes' epic novel, *Don Quixote*, is published
	1620	Pilgrims land at Plymouth Rock, Massachusetts
First Folio, earliest collection of Shakespeare's plays	1623	
A New Way to Pay Old Debts, a satiric comedy by Philip Massinger	1625	

Opening of the Farnese Theater in Parma	1628	William Harvey discovers that blood circulates
Performance of *The Persevering Prince* by Calderón de la Barca, one of Spain's finest playwrights	1629	
Lope de Vega's *San Juan Nights*; Calderón de la Barca's *Life is a Dream*	1631	
Théâtre du Marais opens in Paris under the direction of Montdory, a leading actor of the period	1632	Galileo publishes work supporting Copernicus' theories on the solar system, and the following year he is tried for heresy by the Inquisition
Pierre Corneille's *Le Cid*, first masterpiece of the French classical theater, is performed	1637	
	1643	Louis XIV succeeds to the throne of France
Publication of *Lucifer* by the Dutch writer Joost Vondel; the play receives only two performances before it is banned by the Dutch clergy	1654	
Production in Paris of *Les Précieuses Ridicules* establishes Molière as a leading comic writer	1659	
	1666	John Milton finishes his epic poem *Paradise Lost*
Production of Jean Racine's first drama, *Andromaque*, at the Hôtel du Bourgogne, Paris	1667	
The French clergy finally lifts its ban against Molière's *Tartuffe*, written five years earlier	1669	
Molière collapses during a performance of *The Imaginary Invalid* and dies the same day	1673	
First performance of William Wycherley's Restoration comedy *The Country Wife*	1675	Sir Christopher Wren supervises the rebuilding of fire-damaged St. Paul's Cathedral
Racine's *Phèdre*	1677	
Founding of the Comédie Française	1680	
	1687	Isaac Newton publishes *Principia*, stating fundamental laws of gravity and motion
	1688	Glorious Revolution in England
Racine writes *Esther*, ending a twelve-year separation from the theater; two years later his last major work, *Athalie*, is produced	1689	
The Way of the World by William Congreve; now considered a masterpiece, the play had such a poor run that Congreve retired from the theater	1700	
Love Suicide at Sonezaki by Chikamatsu Monzaemon, leading playwright of the Japanese Bunraku and Kabuki theaters	1703	
The Beaux' Stratagem, last of George Farquhar's comedies, is produced months before his death	1707	
Lesage's *Turcaret* satirizes French social conditions	1709	Louis XIV orders the Port Royal monastery, a center of Jansenism, closed
Francesco Maffei's *Merope*, an outstanding Italian drama that is to serve as a model for Voltaire's *Mérope*, produced in 1743	1713	Signing of the Treaty of Utrecht provides for permanent separation of the thrones of Spain and France
	1721	Bach composes the six *Brandenburg Concertos*
French playwright Pierre Marivau's *La Surprise de l'Amour* done by Comedie-Italienne in Paris	1722	
Voltaire's finest tragedy, *Zaire*, purportedly based on Shakespeare's *Othello*	1736	
	1739	Hume writes *A Treatise on Human Nature*
	1741	Handel completes his most famous oratorio, *Messiah*
La Vedova Scaltra by Carlo Goldoni, whose work supplants commedia dell'arte in Italian theater	1748	
Khorev, the first tragedy written by Alexander Sumarokov, founder of Russian drama	1749	
	1751	Diderot and D'Alembert begin *L'Encyclopédie*
Goldoni's *La Locandiera*	1753	
Gotthold Lessing's *Miss Sarah Sampson*, a drama exploring German middle-class life	1755	
Denis Diderot completes *The Illegitimate Son*, a play not performed until 1771	1757	
	1758	Voltaire publishes *Candide*
Performance of *L'amore delle Tre Melarance* by Carlo Gozzi, who seeks to preserve the influence of commedia dell'arte in Italy	1761	

181

First Polish public theater opens in Warsaw	1765	
Oliver Goldsmith's *She Stoops to Conquer* presented at Covent Garden Theatre in London; *Götz von Berlichingen*, Goethe's first play	1773	
Construction begins on La Scala in Milan	1774	
Production of Pierre Beaumarchais' *The Barber of Seville*; his second play concerning Figaro—*The Marriage of Figaro*—is presented in 1784	1775	
Sturm und Drang by Friedrich Klinger; Emperor Joseph II designates the Burgtheater of Vienna as home of the Austrian National Theater	1776	American Declaration of Independence; Adam Smith's classic economic treatise, *The Wealth of Nations*, published
First performance of Sheridan's *The School for Scandal*, highly popular English comedy	1777	Haydn composes the Symphony in C
Italian poet Vittorio Alfieri's tragedy *Saul*	1781	Kant publishes *The Critique of Pure Reason*
Opening of the National Theater in Berlin	1786	
Ban on French playwright Marie Joseph de Chénier's *Charles IX* lifted; strong performance by Talma heightens the play's antimonarchial theme	1789	Parisians storm the Bastille; Declaration of the Rights of Man proclaimed
	1793-94	Reign of Terror in France
Completion of Schiller's historical trilogy *Wallenstein*; one year later he writes *Maria Stuart*	1799	
	1803	United States purchases Louisiana Territory from France, doubling the new nation's size
Production of Schiller's final play, *Wilhelm Tell*	1804	Napoleon proclaimed emperor of France; Beethoven's Eroica Symphony given first performance
	1805	British defeat French and Spanish forces at the Battle of Trafalgar
Publication of first part of Goethe's masterwork, *Faust*; the second part is published in 1832	1808	
	1814	Congress of Vienna convenes
	1815	Napoleon defeated at Waterloo
Opening of the Odéon theater in Paris	1816	
The Count of Carmagnola by Alessandro Manzoni, a leading novelist of the Italian romantic school	1820	
Alexander Pushkin's historical drama *Boris Godunov*	1825	
Production of Alexander Dumas père's *Henry III and His Court* provides one of the first successes of the romantic theater in France	1829	Balzac begins his masterwork, *The Human Comedy*
Riot follows opening night performance of Victor Hugo's *Hernani* at the Comédie Française in Paris	1830	Stendhal's *The Red and the Black* published
De Vigny's *Chatterton*, one of the most celebrated French romantic dramas	1835	
Gogol's masterpiece, *The Inspector General*, performed at court theater before Tsar Nicholas I	1836	
	1837	Accession of Queen Victoria of England
	1848	Revolutionary movements erupt and are quelled in Germany, Italy, and Austria; abdication of Louis Philippe and proclamation of the Second Republic; Marx and Engels' *The Communist Manifesto*
Première performance of *Adrienne Lecouvreur*, a tragedy written by Scribe and Legouvé for the famous French actress Rachel	1849	Potato famine in Ireland sparks mass migration of Irish to the United States
	1850	Publication of Charles Dickens' *David Copperfield*
Alexander Dumas fils' adaptation of his own novel *La Dame aux Camélias* becomes one of the most popular romantic dramas of the nineteenth century	1852	
	1854	Commodore Perry opens Japan to Western trade
	1857	Gustave Flaubert writes *Madame Bovary*; publication of Charles Baudelaire's *Les Fleurs du Mal*
	1859	Charles Darwin's *On the Origin of Species . . .*
	1863	Battle of Gettysburg, turning point of Civil War
Henrik Ibsen completes his first major verse drama, *Brand*; the following year he writes *Peer Gynt*	1864	
	1866	Fëdor Dostoevski writes *Crime and Punishment*
	1869	Suez Canal completed; Tolstoy's *War and Peace*

Publication of Émile Zola's *Thérèse Raquin*; the play's preface contains an exposition of the basic tenets of theatrical naturalism

1874 — First major exhibition of Impressionist paintings held in Paris

1876 — Richard Wagner's four-opera cycle *Der Ring des Nibelungen* presented at first Bayreuth Festival

First Shakespeare Festival held at Stratford; Ibsen writes *A Doll's House*

1879

August Strindberg publishes *Miss Julie*

1888 — Vincent Van Gogh paints *The Sunflowers*

Production of Ibsen's character study *Hedda Gabler*

1890

Gerhart Hauptmann's masterful naturalistic drama *Die Weber*

1892

First performance of Oscar Wilde's satire *The Importance of Being Earnest*

1895 — Publication of Freud's *Studies on Hysteria* marks the beginning of psychoanalysis

Anton Chekhov's early work *The Seagull* is poorly received; two years later it is successfully revived by the Moscow Art Theater

1896

Edmond Rostand's *Cyrano de Bergerac*—one of the finest romantic plays produced in France

1897

Stanislavsky and Nemirovich-Danchenko found Moscow Art Theater; production of George Bernard Shaw's *Candida*

1898

Italian writer Gabriele D'Annunzio dedicates *La Gioconda* to Eleonora Duse, who scores a personal triumph in the title role; founding of the Abbey Theatre in Dublin by William Butler Yeats and Lady Gregory; Chekhov's *Uncle Vanya*

1899

Production of Chekhov's *The Three Sisters*; Strindberg's *Dance of Death*

1901

Maxim Gorky's *The Lower Depths*

1902

1903 — Orville and Wilbur Wright design the first airplane

Kathleen ni Houlihan, a one-act play by William Butler Yeats; *The Cherry Orchard*, Chekhov's final play

1904

Max Reinhardt is named director of the Deutsches Theater in Berlin

1905

1905-16 — Albert Einstein formulates special and general theories of relativity

Production of *A Flea in Her Ear*, one of more than sixty farces written by Georges Feydeau

1907 — Exhibition of Pablo Picasso's *Les Demoiselles d'Avignon* signals the beginning of the Cubist era

1912 — Chinese Republic established

1913 — Première performance of Igor Stravinsky's *Le Sacre du Printemps*

Shaw's *Pygmalion*

1914 — World War I begins; Panama Canal opens

1916 — D.W. Griffith releases *Birth of a Nation* in theaters across the United States

Cosi e se vi pare ("Right You Are if You Think You Are") an early work of Luigi Pirandello; in 1921 he writes *Six Characters in Search of an Author*

1917 — Russian Revolution

1919 — Treaty of Versailles ends World War I

1922 — James Joyce's *Ulysses* published in France

Sean O'Casey's *Juno and the Paycock*

1924 — First performance of Gershwin's *Rhapsody in Blue*

Pirandello founds Teatro dell'Arte in Rome

1925

Rioting in Dublin follows performance of O'Casey's *The Plough and the Stars* at the Abbey Theatre

1926

Bertolt Brecht and Kurt Weill collaborate on *The Threepenny Opera*

1928 — Discovery of penicillin by the British scientist Alexander Fleming

Elmer's Rice's *Street Scene*, realistic drama of life in the slums, first produced

1929 — Stock market crash on Wall Street leads to worldwide economic depression; Museum of Modern Art founded in New York

Mourning Becomes Electra, Eugene O'Neill's trilogy based upon Aeschylus' *Oresteia*, produced

1931 — Japanese occupy Manchuria

Blood Wedding, first play in a trilogy by Spanish writer Federico Garcia Lorca; the final two plays are *Yerma* and *The House of Bernarda Alba*

1933 — Adolf Hitler becomes chancellor of Germany

French playwright Jean Cocteau's modern version of the Oedipus myth, *La Machine Infernale*

1934

Murder in the Cathedral, a play in verse by the English poet T. S. Eliot; establishment of the Federal Theater—the first nationwide, government-financed theater project in the U.S.	1935
Jean Giraudoux's antiwar drama *Tiger at the Gates*	1936
	1936-39 Spanish Civil War
Production of *Our Town*, Thornton Wilder's portrait of small-town life in America; publication of Antonin Artaud's *Le Théâtre et Son Double*, a collection of essays on the "Theater of Cruelty"	1938
Brecht writes *Mother Courage and Her Children*, but the play is not produced until 1945; Lillian Hellman's *The Little Foxes*	1939 German invasion of Poland begins World War II
	1941 Japanese attack Pearl Harbor and bring United States into World War II
	1942 Enrico Fermi and his colleagues at the University of Chicago produce first fission of uranium
Jean-Paul Sartre's *Les Mouches* performed in Paris in spite of attempts to censor the play by the Nazis; Brecht's *The Good Woman of Setzuan*	1943
Performance of Albert Camus' *Caligula* in Paris; *The Madwoman of Chaillot* by Giraudoux	1945 Allies defeat Hitler's Germany; first atomic bombs used against the Japanese to end World War II in the Pacific; United Nations organized
Tennessee Williams' first Broadway play, *The Glass Menagerie*, marks the comeback of American actress Laurette Taylor; the following year Williams writes *A Streetcar Named Desire*	1946
Julian Beck and Judith Malina organize the Living Theater; Brecht's *Galileo*; first international theatrical festival held in Edinburgh	1947 India gains independence from Great Britain
	1948 State of Israel established
Brecht and Helene Weigel establish a resident acting company in East Berlin called The Berliner Ensemble; Arthur Miller's *Death of a Salesman*	1949 People's Republic of China proclaimed
	1950 Outbreak of the Korean War
Circle in the Square production of *Summer and Smoke* marks opening of off-Broadway theater	1952 Publication of Dylan Thomas' *Collected Poems*
First production of Samuel Beckett's landmark tragicomedy, *Waiting for Godot*, in Paris	1953 British and American scientists decipher the design of the DNA molecule, basis of cell structure
	1954 French defeated at battle of Dienbienphu
John Osborne's drama *Look Back in Anger* introduces the era of "angry young men" to English theater; posthumous production of O'Neill's *Long Day's Journey Into Night*	1956 Suez Canal crisis; Russia crushes uprising in Hungary
	1957 *Sputnik I* launched by the Soviet Union
	1958 Charles de Gaulle elected president of France; establishment of the Fifth Republic
Jack Gelber's study of drug addiction, *The Connection*, presented by the Living Theater	1959
Eugene Ionesco's *Rhinoceros* produced by Jean-Louis Barrault at the Théâtre de France in Paris	1960
Jean Genêt's most ambitious play, *The Screens*, performed in West Berlin	1961 Soviet astronaut Yuri Gagarin becomes first man sent into space; Berlin Wall is built
First production of Edward Albee's *Who's Afraid of Virginia Woolf?*	1962
Joan Littlewood produces *Oh What a Lovely War* at the experimental Theatre Workshop in London	1963 Assassination of President John F. Kennedy
Le Roi Jones' *The Dutchman*	1964
Grotowsky founds the Laboratory Theater in Wroclaw, Poland	1965
Harold Pinter's *The Homecoming*	1967 Arab-Israeli Six-Day War; first surgical transplant of a human heart performed
	1969 American astronauts walk on the moon
Living Theater disbands	1970
Royal Shakespeare Company presents Peter Brooks' staging of *A Midsummer Night's Dream*	1971
Negro Ensemble's production of *The River Niger*	1973 Agreement signed to end the Vietnam War; renewed fighting in the Middle East

Selected Bibliography

Artaud, Antonin. *The Theatre and Its Double.* Translated by Mary C. Richards. New York: Grove Press, 1958.

Baldry, H. C. *The Greek Tragic Theatre.* New York: W. W. Norton, 1973.

Bowers, Faubion. *The Theatre in the East: A Survey of Ancient Dance and Drama.* New York: Grove Press, 1960.

Brecht, Bertolt. *Brecht on Theatre.* Translated and annotated by John Willett. New York: Hill & Wang, 1964.

Brenan, Gerald. *The Literature of the Spanish People.* Second ed. London: Cambridge University Press, 1953.

Brook, Peter. *The Empty Space.* New York: Avon Books, 1969.

Brustein, Robert. *Seasons of Discontent.* New York: Simon & Schuster, 1967.

Chaikin, Joseph. *The Presence of the Actor.* New York: Atheneum Publishers, 1972.

Chamberlain, Eric R. *Everyday Life in Renaissance Times.* New York: G. P. Putnam's Sons, 1967.

Diderot, Denis. *The Paradox of Acting.* New York: Burt Franklin, 1957.

Gage, John. *Life in Italy at the time of the Medici.* Peter Quennell, ed. New York: G. P. Putnam's Sons, 1970.

Gargi, Balwant. *Folk Theatre of India.* Seattle: U. of Washington Press, 1966.

Harbage, Alfred. *Shakespeare's Audience.* Gloucester: Peter Smith, 1969.

Hunnigher, Benjamin. *Origin of Theater.* New York: Hill & Wang, 1961.

Slonim, Marc. *Russian Theatre: From the Empire to the Soviets.* New York: Macmillan, 1962.

Stanislavsky, Constantin. *Stanislavsky on the Art of the Stage.* Translated by David Magarshack. New York: Hill & Wang, 1962.

Picture Credits

Collection, London **139** Bibliothèque Nationale, Paris (Scarnati) **140** Newspaper clipping: Bibliothèque Nationale, Paris (Harlingue-Viollet) *The Brothers Karamazov*: Bibliothèque de l'Arsenal, Collection Rondel, Paris (Lalance) **141** Jacques Copeau: Bibliothèque de l'Arsenal, Paris (Bernand) Max Reinhardt: Theater Museum, Munich

CHAPTER 10 **142** Piccolo Teatro, Milan **144** *Death of a Salesman*: Culver Pictures *Long Day's Journey Into Night*: Museum of the City of New York **145, 146** Museum of the City of New York **147** Private Collection, Paris (Giraudon) **148** Bilderdienst Suddeutscher Verlag, Munich **148-150** (Mulas) **151** (Ciminaghi) **152** (Pino)

MEMOIRS OF THEATRICAL LIVES **154-177** Playbills courtesy of the Walter Hampden Memorial Library

Index